Dynamic Programming
100 Interview Questions

X.Y. Wang

Contents

3 Intermediate   63

4 Advanced   107

Chapter 1

Introduction

Dynamic programming is an essential technique in computer science and has become a cornerstone in the field of algorithm design. It is a problem-solving approach that breaks complex problems down into simpler, overlapping subproblems, and builds up solutions from the smaller subproblems to solve the original problem. This powerful technique enables us to develop efficient algorithms for a wide range of problems, many of which arise frequently in real-world applications.

The primary goal of this book, "Dynamic Programming: 100 Interview Questions", is to provide a comprehensive guide to understanding and mastering dynamic programming, as well as to prepare readers for interviews in the software engineering field. The book is divided into five main sections, progressing from basic concepts to advanced techniques, providing a thorough understanding of dynamic programming at different levels of expertise.

In the first section, we will cover the basics of dynamic programming, discussing its core principles, the differences between top-down and bottom-up approaches, memoization, overlapping subproblems, and the relationship with greedy algorithms. We will also explore practical examples of implementing dynamic programming solutions to problems like the Fibonacci sequence and longest common subsequence.

The second section focuses on intermediate-level dynamic programming topics. We will discuss state space reduction, divide and conquer algorithms, and trade-offs between top-down and bottom-up approaches. This section also features problems like the Rod Cutting problem, Word Break problem, and Matrix Chain Multiplication problem.

The third section delves into advanced dynamic programming concepts, covering topics such as time and space complexity trade-offs, state-transition equations, and state compression. We will work through problems like the Traveling Salesman Problem, Maximum Length Chain of Pairs, and Egg Dropping Puzzle.

The fourth section is dedicated to expert-level topics in dynamic programming. Here, we will explore techniques such as rolling hash, parallelism, and the principle of optimality. Problems covered in this section include Text Justification, Maximum Profit with K Transactions, and Minimum Cost to Merge Stones.

Finally, the fifth section covers guru-level dynamic programming concepts and techniques. We will discuss handling uncertainty, continuous state spaces, and actions in dynamic programming problems. This section features problems like Tree Edit Distance, Optimal Task Assignment with Different Time

Intervals and Constraints, and Resource Allocation with Time Windows and Precedence Constraints.

Each chapter in the book contains a clear explanation of a concept or technique, followed by one or more example problems that illustrate the topic. The solutions are provided with detailed explanations, enabling the reader to grasp the underlying logic and thought process.

Whether you are a student preparing for competitive exams, a professional looking to sharpen your skills, or a job seeker preparing for technical interviews, this book will be an invaluable resource on your journey to mastering dynamic programming. By working through the questions and understanding the solutions, you will develop a strong foundation in dynamic programming and be well-equipped to tackle even the most challenging problems in this domain.

Chapter 2

Basic

2.1 What is dynamic programming and why is it useful?

Dynamic Programming (DP) is a problem-solving technique that involves breaking down complex problems into smaller subproblems and solving them one by one. This approach is useful for solving problems that have overlapping subproblems, meaning that multiple subproblems have the same optimal solution.

The key idea behind DP is to compute the solutions to subproblems only once and store them in memory so that they can be reused later. By doing this, we can avoid redundant computations and dramatically improve the efficiency of our algorithms.

DP is particularly useful for optimization problems, where the goal is to find the best solution among a set of candidate solutions. Examples of problems that can be solved using DP include maximum subarray, longest increasing subsequence, and the knapsack problem.

One common use case for DP is in the field of computer science, where it is used to solve problems in fields such as artificial intelligence, optimization, data analysis, and computational biology. It is also used in fields like economics, engineering, and physics.

Here's an example of how DP can be used to solve the Fibonacci sequence problem:

```
public static int fibonacci(int n) {
    int[] memo = new int[n + 1];
    return fibonacciHelper(n, memo);
}

private static int fibonacciHelper(int n, int[] memo) {
    if (n <= 1) {
        return n;
    }
    if (memo[n] != 0) {
        return memo[n];
    }
    int fib = fibonacciHelper(n - 1, memo) + fibonacciHelper(n - 2,
     memo);
    memo[n] = fib;
    return fib;
}
```

In this example, we use dynamic programming to solve the Fibonacci sequence problem by storing the results of previous Fibonacci calculations in an array called memo. This memoization technique allows us to reuse previously calculated Fibonacci values instead of re-computing them, resulting in a faster and more efficient algorithm.

2.2 Can you explain the differences between top-down and bottom-up dynamic programming?

Dynamic programming is a technique for solving problems by breaking them down into smaller subproblems and solving them recursively. Both top-down and bottom-up dynamic programming use this approach, but they differ in the order in which the subproblems are solved.

Top-Down Dynamic Programming:

Top-down dynamic programming (also known as memoization) begins by breaking down the original problem into smaller subproblems, similar to bottom-up dynamic programming, but it solves each subproblem recursively, from the top of the problem tree to the bottom, before moving on to the next subproblem. In this approach, we store the solutions to subproblems in a lookup table (also called memoization table) so that we don't have to re-compute them every time they are needed. This helps to avoid redundant computations and reduce the time complexity of the algorithm.

A classic example of a problem that can be solved using top-down dynamic programming is the Fibonacci sequence. Here's what the top-down implementation in Java would look like:

```java
public int fibonacci(int n, int[] memo) {
  if (n <= 1) {
    return n;
  }
  if (memo[n] != 0) {
    return memo[n];
  }
  memo[n] = fibonacci(n-1, memo) + fibonacci(n-2, memo);
  return memo[n];
```

```
}
```

Bottom-Up Dynamic Programming:

Bottom-up dynamic programming, on the other hand, begins by breaking down the original problem into smaller subproblems and solves them iteratively, from the smallest subproblem to the largest, gradually building up to the solution of the original problem. In this approach, we typically use an array to store the solutions to subproblems, with each element representing the solution to a specific subproblem. This can be more efficient than the top-down approach in terms of both time and memory complexity.

Let's modify our Fibonacci example to use the bottom-up approach in Java:

```java
public int fibonacci(int n) {
  if (n <= 1) {
    return n;
  }
  int[] memo = new int[n+1];
  memo[0] = 0;
  memo[1] = 1;
  for (int i = 2; i <= n; i++) {
    memo[i] = memo[i-1] + memo[i-2];
  }
  return memo[n];
}
```

In summary, while both top-down and bottom-up dynamic programming use the same approach of breaking down problems into smaller subproblems, they differ in the order in which the subproblems are solved. Top-down solves subproblems recursively from top to bottom, while bottom-up solves subproblems iteratively from bottom to top. The choice between them depends on the specific problem at hand and the efficiencies required.

2.3   What is memoization and how is it used in dynamic programming?

Memoization is a technique in dynamic programming where the results of expensive function calls are cached or stored to avoid redundant calculations. It is a top-down approach of dynamic programming.

In more technical terms, memoization is an optimization technique where the result of a function call is stored in memory so that subsequent calls with the same inputs can be returned from the cache instead of recalculating the results.

Dynamic programming, on the other hand, is a bottom-up approach that breaks down a problem into smaller subproblems to solve them recursively. The solutions to the subproblems are then combined to solve the larger problem.

Memoization can be used in dynamic programming to optimize the time complexity of a recursive solution. When solving a problem recursively, there is a possibility that the same subproblem will be solved multiple times. By memoizing the results of these subproblems, we can avoid solving them repeatedly and thereby reduce the time complexity of the code.

Heres an example Java code that implements memoization in a dynamic programming solution to compute the nth Fibonacci number:

```java
import java.util.*;

public class Fibonacci {

    static Map<Integer, Integer> memo = new HashMap<>();

    public static int fibonacci(int n) {
        if (n <= 1) {
```

```
            return n;
        } else if (memo.containsKey(n)) {
            return memo.get(n);
        } else {
            int result = fibonacci(n - 1) + fibonacci(n - 2);
            memo.put(n, result);
            return result;
        }
    }

    public static void main(String[] args) {
        System.out.println(fibonacci(6)); // Output: 8
    }
}
```

In this code, we use a 'Map' to store the results of previous function calls using memoization. Each time the 'fibonacci' function is called with a value of 'n', we first check if the result has already been memoized using 'memo.containsKey(n)'. If so, we simply return the memoized result using 'memo.get(n)'. Otherwise, we compute the result recursively and store it in the 'Map' using 'memo.put(n, result)'.

By using memoization, we avoid calculating the same Fibonacci numbers multiple times and greatly improve the performance of our code, especially for large values of 'n'.

2.4   How do you determine if a problem can be solved using dynamic programming?

To determine if a problem can be solved using dynamic programming, we usually look for two main properties:

1. **Optimal Substructure** - if a problem can be broken down into smaller subproblems and the optimal solution for the

original problem can be constructed efficiently from the optimal solutions of its subproblems, then the problem exhibits optimal substructure. In other words, the problem can be solved using a recursive approach where the solution to the original problem depends on the solutions to its subproblems. This is a key property for dynamic programming and it allows us to apply memoization or tabulation to avoid redundant computations.

2. **Overlapping Subproblems** - if the subproblems required to solve the original problem recur repeatedly, then the problem exhibits overlapping subproblems. In other words, the same subproblems are being solved multiple times during the computation of the solution. This can result in redundant computations that can be avoided using dynamic programming.

Once we have established that a problem exhibits these two properties, we can consider solving it using dynamic programming by either using the top-down approach (memoization) or the bottom-up approach (tabulation).

For example, let's consider the problem of finding the n-th Fibonacci number given n. This problem exhibits both optimal substructure and overlapping subproblems. The n-th Fibonacci number can be computed recursively as the sum of the (n-1)th and (n-2)th Fibonacci numbers. In other words, the solution to the original problem depends on the solutions to its subproblems. Additionally, the computation of the (n-1)th and (n-2)th Fibonacci numbers are subproblems that are repeated multiple times during the computation of the solution for the original problem.

Here is an example code for computing the n-th Fibonacci number using dynamic programming (bottom-up approach or tabulation) in Java:

```java
public static int fibonacci(int n) {
    if(n == 0) {
        return 0;
    }
    if(n == 1 || n == 2) {
        return 1;
    }
    int[] fib = new int[n+1];
    fib[1] = 1;
    fib[2] = 1;
    for(int i=3; i<=n; i++) {
        fib[i] = fib[i-1] + fib[i-2];
    }
    return fib[n];
}
```

In this code, we are storing the solutions to the subproblems (i.e., the ith Fibonacci number) in an array called fib. We start by initializing fib[1] and fib[2] to 1 (since they are base cases). We then use a loop to compute fib[i] as the sum of fib[i-1] and fib[i-2]. Finally, we return fib[n], which is the solution to the original problem. This code runs in $O(n)$ time and $O(n)$ space, which is much faster than the naive recursive approach that runs in $O(2^n)$ time.

2.5 Can you explain the concept of overlapping subproblems in dynamic programming?

The overlapping subproblems is one of the key features of dynamic programming that allow us to solve complex algorithms efficiently.

In general, dynamic programming is used to solve problems by breaking them down into smaller subproblems and recursively solving them while keeping track of the solutions to avoid duplicating work. These smaller subproblems might be related to each other and might be solved recursively using the same algorithms.

In dynamic programming, overlapping subproblems occur when we have to solve the same subproblem multiple times. In other words, they occur when two or more subproblems share a common solution or a common computation. This would result in duplicate work and slow down the algorithm.

To avoid this issue, we use a technique called memoization or tabulation in dynamic programming. Memoization or tabulation stores the solution to a subproblem so that if we encounter the same subproblem again, we can simply look up the solution without having to solve the subproblem repeatedly. This technique significantly reduces the time complexity of our solution.

Here is an example of the Fibonacci sequence to illustrate the concept of overlapping subproblems:

```
public static int fibonacci(int n){
    if(n == 0){
        return 0;
    } else if(n == 1){
        return 1;
    } else{
        return fibonacci(n-1) + fibonacci(n-2);
    }
}
```

The above code solves for the nth term of the Fibonacci sequence using recursion. However, this approach suffers from a serious performance issue. For larger values of n, the same subproblem is calculated over and over again, resulting in duplicate work. This means that the same value is calculated multiple times.

Dynamic programming solves this issue by storing the result of solved subproblems in a table or array. The below code does this using tabulation:

```
public static int fibonacci(int n){
    if(n == 0){
        return 0;
    } else if(n == 1){
        return 1;
    }

    int[] memo = new int[n+1];
    memo[0] = 0;
    memo[1] = 1;

    for(int i=2; i<=n; i++){
        memo[i] = memo[i-1] + memo[i-2];
    }

    return memo[n];
}
```

The above code uses dynamic programming to solve the Fibonacci sequence by creating an array to store the results of solved subproblems. We perform a loop from 2 to n and store the Fibonacci value of each subproblem in the memo array. If we encounter the same subproblem again, we simply look up its value in the memo array without having to recalculate it. This avoids duplicating work and makes the algorithm more efficient.

2.6   What is the difference between greedy algorithms and dynamic programming?

Greedy algorithms and dynamic programming are both optimization techniques commonly used in algorithm design. Although both approaches aim to solve optimization problems, they differ in their methodologies and the types of problems they are suited for.

Greedy algorithms make locally optimal choices at each step of the algorithm in the hopes of finding a global optimum. In other words, at each stage, the algorithm selects the best available option without considering the future consequences of that decision. Greedy algorithms are typically easy to design and implement, with lower computational overhead than dynamic programming. However, they often do not produce the optimal solution, and in some cases, they may not even produce a feasible solution.

Dynamic programming, on the other hand, breaks down a complex problem into smaller subproblems and solves each subproblem exactly once. It then uses the solutions to these subproblems to construct the solution of the original problem. Unlike greedy algorithms, the optimal solution may not always be apparent, and dynamic programming may require significant computational overhead to solve large problems. However, they generally produce the correct solution and are more versatile in handling a wide range of optimization problems.

For example, let's consider the problem of making change. Given a list of denominations, what is the minimum number of coins needed to make a certain amount of change? A greedy algorithm might start with the largest denomination and work its way down, taking as many of each denomination as possible until the desired amount is reached. However, this approach does not always produce the optimal solution. For example, suppose the denominations are 1, 7, 10 and the desired amount is 15. The greedy algorithm would select one coin of denomination 10 and five coins of denomination 1, for a total of six coins. However, the optimal solution is to use three coins of denomination 5, which yields a total of three coins.

In contrast, dynamic programming can solve this problem optimally by breaking it down into subproblems. Let C(i) be the minimum number of coins needed to make change for i. Then we can write:

```
C(i) = min(C(i-d) + 1), where d is a denomination and i >= d
```

In other words, the minimum number of coins needed to make change for i is equal to the minimum of the number of coins needed to make change for i minus each denomination, plus one coin for that denomination. By computing C(i) for all i up to the desired amount, we can determine the optimal solution. This approach is more computationally expensive than the greedy algorithm, but it produces the correct answer for any denomination set and desired amount.

2.7   Implement the Fibonacci sequence using dynamic programming with a bottom-up approach.

The Fibonacci sequence is a sequence of numbers in which each number after the first two is the sum of the two preceding ones. In mathematical terms, it can be defined as:

```
F(n) = F(n-1) + F(n-2), where F(0) = 0 and F(1) = 1.
```

A straightforward recursive solution to this problem looks like this:

```
int fibonacci(int n) {
    if (n <= 1) {
        return n;
    }
    return fibonacci(n - 1) + fibonacci(n - 2);
}
```

However, this solution is inefficient for large values of n since it recomputes the same values multiple times. Dynamic programming can help us improve the efficiency of this algorithm by storing the results of previously computed values and reusing them if necessary.

Here's the bottom-up approach to implementing the Fibonacci sequence using dynamic programming:

```
public static int fibonacci(int n) {
    if (n <= 1) {
        return n;
    }

    int[] memo = new int[n + 1];
    memo[0] = 0;
    memo[1] = 1;

    for (int i = 2; i <= n; i++) {
        memo[i] = memo[i - 1] + memo[i - 2];
    }

    return memo[n];
}
```

In this solution, we create an array called memo to store the results of previously computed Fibonacci numbers. We start by initializing memo[0] and memo[1] to their respective values in the sequence.

We then use a loop to iterate from i=2 up to n, computing and storing each new Fibonacci number in the memo array. By the time we reach the end of the loop, memo[n] will contain the desired Fibonacci number.

This approach has a time complexity of $O(n)$ and a space complexity of $O(n)$, which is more efficient than the recursive approach discussed earlier.

2.8   Implement the Fibonacci sequence using dynamic programming with a top-down approach.

To implement the Fibonacci sequence using dynamic programming with a top-down approach, we can use memoization technique. Memoization is an optimization technique that stores the results of expensive function calls and returns the cached result when the same inputs occur again.

Using memoization, we can avoid repetitive calculations and reduce the time complexity of the algorithm. In the case of the Fibonacci sequence, we can recursively calculate the Fibonacci numbers and store their results in an array or a HashMap. This way, we can avoid calculating the same Fibonacci numbers multiple times.

Here is the Java code for implementing the Fibonacci sequence using dynamic programming with a top-down approach:

```java
public class FibonacciDP {

    private static Map<Integer, Integer> memo = new HashMap<>();

    public static int fib(int n) {
        if (n <= 1) {
            return n;
        }
        if (memo.containsKey(n)) {
            return memo.get(n);
        }
        int result = fib(n-1) + fib(n-2);
```

```
        memo.put(n, result);
        return result;
    }

    public static void main(String[] args) {
        int n = 10;
        for (int i = 0; i <= n; i++) {
            System.out.print(fib(i) + "␣");
        }
    }
}
```

In this code, we have defined a private static HashMap called
memo that will store the Fibonacci numbers that we have already computed. The fib() method takes an integer argument
n and returns the nth Fibonacci number. If n is less than
or equal to 1, the method returns n. Otherwise, it checks if
memo already contains the value of n. If so, it returns that
value. Otherwise, it recursively calculates the nth Fibonacci
number using the formula fib(n-1) + fib(n-2), stores the result
in memo, and returns the result.

In the main method, we have defined n as 10, and we are calling
the fib() method for each value of i from 0 to 10. The output
of this code will be:

0 1 1 2 3 5 8 13 21 34 55

As we can see, the Fibonacci numbers have been calculated
using dynamic programming with a top-down approach, and
the results have been cached in memo to avoid repetitive calculations. This approach has a time complexity of $O(n)$, where
n is the index of the Fibonacci number we want to calculate.

2.9   Can you provide an example of a problem that can be solved using both greedy algorithms and dynamic programming?

One classic example of a problem that can be solved using both greedy algorithms and dynamic programming is the "coin change" problem.

The problem statement goes as follows: Given a target amount of money and a set of coin denominations, what is the minimum number of coins needed to make up the target amount? For example, if the target amount is 11 and the coin denominations are [1, 5, 10], the answer should be 2 (one 5-cent coin and six 1-cent coins).

One possible solution using the greedy approach is to always pick the largest coin denomination that is less than or equal to the remaining amount. This strategy is known as the "coin denomination sorting" algorithm. While this algorithm can provide a correct solution for many cases, it may fail for certain inputs. For instance, if the coin denominations are [1, 3, 4] and the target amount is 6, the algorithm would return 2 (two 3-cent coins), whereas the optimal solution is 2 (one 4-cent coin and two 1-cent coins).

On the other hand, the problem can also be solved using dynamic programming. One possible approach is to build an array of size (target_amount + 1), where each element represents the minimum number of coins needed to make up the corresponding amount. The base case is when the amount is zero, which requires zero coins. For each amount, we iterate

over all possible coin denominations and compute the minimum
number of coins required by taking the minimum of (current
minimum) and (minimum for the remaining amount plus one
coin). The final answer is the value at array[target_amount].

Here's an implementation of the dynamic programming solution in Java:

```java
public static int coinChange(int[] coins, int amount) {
    int[] dp = new int[amount + 1];
    Arrays.fill(dp, amount + 1);
    dp[0] = 0;
    for (int i = 1; i <= amount; i++) {
        for (int j = 0; j < coins.length; j++) {
            if (coins[j] <= i) {
                dp[i] = Math.min(dp[i], dp[i - coins[j]] + 1);
            }
        }
    }
    return dp[amount] > amount ? -1 : dp[amount];
}
```

As we can see, the dynamic programming solution guarantees
the optimal solution for any set of coin denominations and
target amount, while the greedy algorithm may fail for some
cases. However, the dynamic programming solution requires
more space and time complexity than the greedy algorithm,
especially for large inputs or non-uniform coin denominations.
Therefore, the choice of solution depends on the trade-off between optimality and efficiency in a given scenario.

2.10   What are the key steps to solve a dynamic programming problem?

The key steps to solve a dynamic programming problem are:

1. Understanding the problem and defining the subproblems: Before starting to solve a dynamic programming problem, it is important to understand the problem statement and define its subproblems. Subproblems are smaller versions of the original problem that can be solved recursively or iteratively. For example, in the Fibonacci sequence problem, the subproblems are calculating the values of Fibonacci series until n-1 and n-2.

2. Deciding on the state representation: The state representation is a way of representing subproblems. The state can be identified by variables such as an index, a length, or a subset of items. For example, in the knapsack problem, the state is represented by weight and the remaining capacity of the knapsack.

3. Formulating the recursive relation: The recursive relation defines the solution of a subproblem in terms of its smaller subproblems. This is the most important step in dynamic programming. It involves identifying how the solution to the subproblem can be expressed in terms of the solution to smaller subproblems. For example, in the Fibonacci sequence problem, the recursive relation can be defined as $F(n) = F(n-1) + F(n-2)$.

4. Identifying the base cases: Base cases are the smallest subproblems that can be directly solved. These are necessary to stop the recursion and provide a solution to the original problem. For example, in the Fibonacci sequence problem, the base cases are $F(0) = 0$ and $F(1) = 1$.

5. Constructing the solution: After solving the subproblems, we can construct the solution to the original problem using the results of the subproblems. For example, in the Fibonacci sequence problem, the solution is $F(n)$.

6. Adding memorization or tabulation: To improve the efficiency of dynamic programming solutions, memoization or
tabulation techniques can be used to reduce redundant computations. Memoization involves storing the results of solved
subproblems in a table or array to avoid recomputing them,
while tabulation involves solving all subproblems in a bottom-
up approach and storing the results in a table or array.

Here is an example code in Java that implements the above
steps to solve the Fibonacci sequence problem:

```java
public int fibonacci(int n) {
    int[] cache = new int[n+1];
    return fibonacciSub(n, cache);
}

public int fibonacciSub(int n, int[] cache) {
    if(n < 2) {
        return n;
    }
    if(cache[n] != 0) {
        return cache[n];
    }
    int result = fibonacciSub(n-1, cache) + fibonacciSub(n-2, cache);
    cache[n] = result;
    return result;
}
```

In this code, we first define a memoization cache to store the
results of subproblems. Then we define the recursive function
'fibonacciSub' that takes the input 'n' and the memoization
cache 'cache'. The base case is when 'n' is less than 2, where
we simply return 'n'. Next, we check whether the solution
to the subproblem has already been computed and stored in
the cache. If it is present in the cache, we simply return the
result. Otherwise, we recursively solve the subproblems and
store the result in the cache before returning it. Finally, we
define 'fibonacci' function that calls 'fibonacciSub' and returns
its result.

2.11   Solve the problem of finding the longest common subsequence (LCS) of two strings using dynamic programming.

The Longest Common Subsequence (LCS) problem is a classic problem in computer science. Given two strings 's1' and 's2', the task is to find the longest common subsequence of the two strings.

A subsequence is a sequence that can be derived from another sequence by deleting some or no elements without changing the order of the remaining elements.

For example, if 's1' = "ABCD" and 's2' = "ACDB", then the LCS of 's1' and 's2' is "ACD".

One approach to solving this problem is by using dynamic programming. The basic idea is to construct a 2D array 'dp[len1+1][len2+1]', where 'len1' and 'len2' are the lengths of 's1' and 's2', respectively. The value of 'dp[i][j]' represents the length of the LCS of the first 'i' characters of 's1' and the first 'j' characters of 's2'.

We can fill up the 'dp' array iteratively, starting from the base cases where one of the strings is empty (i.e., 'dp[i][0]' or 'dp[0][j]' equals 0), and then filling up the rest of the array.

The key observation is that if the last characters of 's1' and 's2' match, then the LCS of the two strings must include that character. Otherwise, the LCS can either include the last character of 's1' or the last character of 's2', but not both.

Therefore, the recurrence relation for computing 'dp[i][j]' is:

```
if s1[i-1] == s2[j-1]:
    dp[i][j] = dp[i-1][j-1] + 1
else:
    dp[i][j] = max(dp[i-1][j], dp[i][j-1])
```

The final answer will be stored in 'dp[len1][len2]'.

Here's an example implementation of the LCS algorithm in Java:

```java
public static String LCS(String s1, String s2) {
    int len1 = s1.length(), len2 = s2.length();
    int[][] dp = new int[len1 + 1][len2 + 1];

    for (int i = 1; i <= len1; i++) {
        for (int j = 1; j <= len2; j++) {
            if (s1.charAt(i - 1) == s2.charAt(j - 1)) {
                dp[i][j] = dp[i - 1][j - 1] + 1;
            } else {
                dp[i][j] = Math.max(dp[i - 1][j], dp[i][j - 1]);
            }
        }
    }

    StringBuilder sb = new StringBuilder();
    int i = len1, j = len2;
    while (i > 0 && j > 0) {
        if (s1.charAt(i - 1) == s2.charAt(j - 1)) {
            sb.append(s1.charAt(i - 1));
            i--;
            j--;
        } else if (dp[i - 1][j] > dp[i][j - 1]) {
            i--;
        } else {
            j--;
        }
    }

    return sb.reverse().toString();
}
```

In this implementation, we first compute the 'dp' array as described above, and then use it to construct the LCS string by following the backtrack process. The backtrack process starts from the bottom-right corner of the 'dp' array and moves up-

wards and/or leftwards depending on the values of 'dp[i-1][j]'
and 'dp[i][j-1]'. Finally, we reverse the string and return it as
the output.

2.12   Solve the problem of finding the shortest common supersequence (SCS) of two strings using dynamic programming.

The problem of finding the shortest common supersequence
(SCS) of two strings can be solved using dynamic programming. An SCS of two strings A and B is a string that contains
both A and B as subsequences, and has the minimum possible
length.

Let's define a function S(i,j) as the length of the SCS of the
substrings A[0:i] and B[0:j]. Using this definition, we can recursively define the value of S(i,j) using the following recurrence
relation:

S(i,j) = 0, if i=0 or j=0 (i.e. if one of the strings is empty, their
SCS is the other string)

S(i,j) = S(i-1, j-1) + 1, if A[i-1] = B[j-1] (i.e. if the last characters
of A and B are the same, we can add that character to the SCS)

S(i,j) = min(S(i-1, j), S(i, j-1)) + 1, otherwise (i.e. if the last
characters of A and B are different, we need to choose between the
two options: add the last character of A or add the last character
of B)

The base case of the recurrence is when one or both strings
are empty, in which case their SCS is simply the other string.

Otherwise, we handle two cases: either the last characters of A and B are the same, in which case we can add that character to the SCS, or they are different, in which case we have to choose which string to add to the SCS. The optimal choice is the one that leads to the shortest SCS.

We can apply this recurrence relation to compute $S(n,m)$, where n and m are the lengths of strings A and B, respectively. The value of $S(n,m)$ gives us the length of the SCS of A and B. However, it doesn't give us the actual SCS. To obtain the SCS, we can use the following algorithm:

```
1. Initialize i=n and j=m.
2. Initialize an empty string result.
3. While i>0 and j>0, do the following:
   * If A[i-1]=B[j-1], add A[i-1] (or B[j-1], it doesn't matter) to
     the beginning of the result, and decrement both i and j.
   * Otherwise, compare S(i-1,j) and S(i,j-1). If S(i-1,j) is
     smaller, add A[i-1] to the beginning of the result and decrement
     i; otherwise add B[j-1] to the beginning of the result and
     decrement j.
4. Add the remaining characters of A or B, whichever is not empty, to
   the beginning of the result.
5. Reverse the result to get the actual SCS.
```

Here's the Java code that implements the above algorithm:

```java
public static String shortestCommonSupersequence(String A, String B)
    {
    int n = A.length();
    int m = B.length();
    int[][] S = new int[n+1][m+1];

    // Initialize base cases
    for (int i=0; i<=n; i++) S[i][0] = 0;
    for (int j=0; j<=m; j++) S[0][j] = 0;

    // Compute S(i,j) using the recurrence
    for (int i=1; i<=n; i++) {
        for (int j=1; j<=m; j++) {
            if (A.charAt(i-1)==B.charAt(j-1)) {
                S[i][j] = S[i-1][j-1] + 1;
            } else {
                S[i][j] = Math.min(S[i-1][j], S[i][j-1]) + 1;
            }
        }
    }
```

```
    }

    // Reconstruct the SCS from S
    int i=n, j=m;
    StringBuilder sb = new StringBuilder();
    while (i>0 && j>0) {
        if (A.charAt(i-1)==B.charAt(j-1)) {
            sb.append(A.charAt(i-1));
            i--;
            j--;
        } else {
            if (S[i-1][j] < S[i][j-1]) {
                sb.append(A.charAt(i-1));
                i--;
            } else {
                sb.append(B.charAt(j-1));
                j--;
            }
        }
    }
    while (i>0) {
        sb.append(A.charAt(i-1));
        i--;
    }
    while (j>0) {
        sb.append(B.charAt(j-1));
        j--;
    }

    return sb.reverse().toString();
}
```

The time complexity of this dynamic programming solution is O(nm), where n and m are the lengths of strings A and B, respectively. This is because we need to compute S(i,j) for all i in 0,1,...,n and all j in 0,1,...,m, which takes O(nm) time. The space complexity is also O(nm), because we need to store the entire S array.

2.13   What is the time complexity of a typical dynamic programming algorithm? Explain with an example.

The time complexity of a typical dynamic programming algorithm depends on several factors such as the size of the input, the number of subproblems, and the amount of computation required for solving each subproblem.

In general, dynamic programming algorithms have a time complexity of $O(n * m)$ where n is the size of the input and m is the number of subproblems. However, some dynamic programming problems may have a time complexity of $O(n^3)$ or even higher.

Let's consider the classic example of the Fibonacci sequence which can be solved using dynamic programming. The Fibonacci sequence is a sequence of numbers in which each number is the sum of the two preceding ones. The first two numbers in the sequence are 0 and 1.

The naive recursive algorithm for computing the nth Fibonacci number has a time complexity of $O(2^n)$ which is very inefficient for large values of n. However, we can solve the problem using dynamic programming by computing the smaller subproblems first and then reusing their results to compute the larger subproblems.

Here's the Java code for solving the Fibonacci sequence using dynamic programming:

```
public static int fib(int n) {
    int[] memo = new int[n + 1];
    memo[0] = 0;
```

```
    memo[1] = 1;
    for (int i = 2; i <= n; i++) {
        memo[i] = memo[i - 1] + memo[i - 2];
    }
    return memo[n];
}
```

In this code, we create an array of size n+1 to store the results of the subproblems. We initialize the first two elements of the array with the base cases of the problem. Then, we use a for loop to compute the ith Fibonacci number by adding the (i-1)th and (i-2)th Fibonacci numbers together.

The time complexity of this algorithm is O(n) because we need to solve n subproblems, and each subproblem takes constant time. Therefore, the dynamic programming solution is much faster than the recursive solution for large values of n.

In summary, the time complexity of a typical dynamic programming algorithm depends on the number of subproblems, the amount of computation required for solving each subproblem, and the size of the input. However, dynamic programming algorithms are often much faster than other algorithms for solving complex optimization problems.

2.14   Implement the Coin Change problem (minimum number of coins) using dynamic programming.

The Coin Change problem is a classic problem in computer science and can be solved using dynamic programming. The problem statement is as follows:

Given a set of coins and a target amount, find the minimum number of coins required to make up the target amount. Assume that there are unlimited coins of each denomination.

For example, if the input is coins = [1, 5, 10, 25] and the target amount is 36, the minimum number of coins required is 3 (one quarter and two dimes).

To solve this problem using dynamic programming, we can use a bottom-up approach where we build a table to keep track of the minimum number of coins required for each target amount.

Let's begin with declaring an array or a map that will hold the minimum number of coins required for each target value. We can initialize the array with maxValue value for all target values except for zero, which requires zero coins to make up.

```
int[] minCoins = new int[target + 1];
Arrays.fill(minCoins, Integer.MAX_VALUE);
minCoins[0] = 0;
```

Next, we can iterate through all possible target values and for each target value, we can iterate through all the available coins. We can use the following recurrence relation to compute the minimum number of coins required for a particular target value:

```
minCoins[target] = min(minCoins[target], 1 + minCoins[target - coin])
```

The above formula means that the minimum number of coins required to make up the target value is the minimum of the previous minimum required coins for that target value or 1 added to the minimum number of coins required to make up the difference between the target value and the coin denomination.

Here is the complete implementation of the dynamic programming solution:

```java
public int coinChange(int[] coins, int amount) {
    int[] minCoins = new int[amount + 1];
    Arrays.fill(minCoins, Integer.MAX_VALUE);
    minCoins[0] = 0;

    for (int i = 1; i <= amount; i++) {
        for (int coin : coins) {
            if (coin <= i && minCoins[i - coin] != Integer.MAX_VALUE)
    {
                minCoins[i] = Math.min(minCoins[i], 1 + minCoins[i -
    coin]);
            }
        }
    }

    return minCoins[amount] == Integer.MAX_VALUE ? -1 : minCoins[
    amount];
}
```

The time complexity of this solution is O(amount * number of coins) and the space complexity is O(amount).

2.15 Solve the 0/1 Knapsack problem using dynamic programming.

The 0/1 Knapsack problem is a classic problem in computer science that is used to determine the most profitable way to fill a knapsack of limited capacity from a set of items with values and weights.

The problem can be stated as follows: given a set of items, each with a weight and a value, determine the number of each item to include in a collection so that the total weight is less than or equal to a given limit, and the total value is as large as possible. The constraint here is that each item can be included in the collection at most once (hence the name "0/1" Knapsack problem).

To solve this problem using dynamic programming, we can use a bottom-up approach by building a table that represents the maximum value that can be obtained by taking i items, with a maximum weight of j.

The steps to solve the problem using dynamic programming are as follows:

1. Initialize a table of size [N+1][W+1]. Here N is the number of items and W is the maximum weight capacity of the knapsack.

2. For each row in the table (representing increasing number of items), and for each column in the table (representing increasing weight capacity), calculate the maximum value of including the i-th item or excluding it.

3. The value of the cell [i][j] will be the maximum of two cases: - The maximum value obtained by including the i-th item and excluding it. - The maximum value obtained by excluding the i-th item and keeping the knapsack's weight capacity same.

4. Once the table is completely filled, the value in the bottom-right corner of the table represents the maximum value that can be obtained using all the items and given weight capacity.

5. To determine which items were included in the collection, we can backtrack through the table by starting at the bottom-right corner, and examining the cells in the row and column that led to the current cell. If the value in the current cell is not equal to the value in the cell above it, then the i-th item was included in the collection. Otherwise, the i-th item was not included.

Let's take a look at an example to illustrate the approach above.

Example: Suppose we have five items, each with a weight and a value as shown below:

```
| Item | Weight | Value |
|------|--------|-------|
| A    | 2      | 3     |
| B    | 3      | 4     |
| C    | 4      | 5     |
| D    | 5      | 8     |
| E    | 9      | 10    |
```

Let's assume that the maximum weight capacity of the knapsack is 10.

To solve this problem using dynamic programming, we can follow the steps outlined above.

Step 1: Create the table.

We create a table of size $[N+1][W+1]$ and initialize it to 0.

```
int[][] table = new int[N+1][W+1];
```

Step 2: Fill the table with maximum value in each cell.

```
for (int i = 1; i <= N; i++) {
  for (int j = 1; j <= W; j++) {
    if (items[i-1].weight > j) {
      table[i][j] = table[i-1][j];
    } else {
      table[i][j] = Math.max(table[i-1][j], table[i-1][j-items[i-1].
      weight] + items[i-1].value);
    }
  }
}
```

Step 3: Determine maximum value

The maximum value that can be obtained is given by the value
in the last cell of the table:

```
int maxVal = table[N][W];
```

Step 4: Determine the items in the collection.

We can backtrack through the table to determine which items
were included in the collection.

```
int i = N;
int j = W;
while (i > 0 && maxVal > 0) {
  if (maxVal != table[i-1][j]) {
    System.out.println("Item " + i + " is included in the collection"
    );
    maxVal -= items[i-1].value;
    j -= items[i-1].weight;
  }
  i--;
}
```

The output of this code will be:

```
Item 2 is included in the collection
Item 3 is included in the collection
Item 4 is included in the collection
```

Therefore, to obtain the maximum value, we need to include
items B, C, and D in the knapsack.

2.16   What is the role of the state-transition equation in dynamic programming? Give an example.

The state-transition equation is a crucial component of dynamic programming, as it defines the recursive relationship

between subproblems in the optimal substructure. In essence, the state-transition equation represents the optimal solution for a given subproblem in terms of the optimal solutions to its smaller subproblems.

For example, consider the Knapsack Problem, where we have a set of items with given values and weights, and we want to find the maximum value we can obtain by selecting a subset of these items subject to a weight constraint. The state-transition equation for this problem takes the following form:

```
knapsack(i, w) = max(knapsack(i-1, w), knapsack(i-1, w-wi) + vi)
```

where 'knapsack(i, w)' represents the maximum value we can obtain by selecting items from the first 'i' items with a weight constraint of 'w', 'wi' and 'vi' denote the weight and value of the 'i-th' item, and we can choose to either include the 'i-th' item or not.

Here, the state-transition equation tells us that the optimal solution for the entire problem depends on the optimal solutions to its smaller subproblems, namely, the maximum value we can obtain by selecting items from the first 'i-1' items with a weight constraint of 'w' (if we don't include the 'i-th' item) and the maximum value we can obtain by selecting items from the first 'i-1' items with a weight constraint of 'w-wi' (if we do include the 'i-th' item). We take the maximum of these two options to obtain the optimal solution for the subproblem 'knapsack(i, w)'.

Overall, the state-transition equation is a powerful tool in dynamic programming that enables us to formalize and solve complex optimization problems by breaking them down into smaller subproblems and recursively combining their optimal solutions.

2.17   Implement a dynamic programming solution for the Longest Increasing Subsequence (LIS) problem.

The Longest Increasing Subsequence (LIS) problem refers to finding the length of the longest subsequence in an array or sequence such that all elements of the subsequence are sorted in increasing order.

The traditional approach for solving this problem involves using recursion and exploring all possible subsequences in the input array. However, this approach is inefficient since it leads to an exponential runtime complexity.

Dynamic programming is a better approach for solving the LIS problem. The idea behind dynamic programming is to avoid redundant and repeated calculations by storing results of subproblems in a table and using them to solve larger problems.

Here's how we can use dynamic programming to solve the LIS problem:

1. Define the problem scope: The problem is to find the length of the longest increasing subsequence in the array.

2. Define the state: The state in this problem can be defined as the length of the longest increasing subsequence from index 0 to i in the input array.

3. Define the base case: The base case is when i=0, which

means the length of the LIS is 1 since there's only one element in the subsequence.

4. Define the recurrence relation: The recurrence relation is the formula for calculating the length of the LIS at any index i in the input array. We can calculate the LIS value for given index, by looping over all previous indexes $j<i$, and checking if the jth value is less than the ith value. If it is less, add 1 to the LIS value for the jth index, and compare it with the LIS value for the ith index. If it's greater than the current LIS value, update the LIS value for the ith index.

5. Calculate the final result: The final result is the maximum value in the LIS table.

Here's a sample implementation of the dynamic programming solution for the LIS problem in Java:

```java
public int lengthOfLIS(int[] nums) {
    int[] lis = new int[nums.length];
    lis[0] = 1;
    int maxLength = 1;
    for (int i = 1; i < nums.length; i++) {
        int maxVal = 0;
        for (int j = 0; j < i; j++) {
            if (nums[j] < nums[i]) {
                maxVal = Math.max(maxVal, lis[j]);
            }
        }
        lis[i] = maxVal + 1;
        maxLength = Math.max(maxLength, lis[i]);
    }
    return maxLength;
}
```

In this implementation, we define an array lis where lis[i] represents the length of the LIS ending at index i in the input array. We initialize lis[0] to 1 since the base case is when i = 0.

We then loop over the input array, and for each index i, we loop over all previous indexes j<i and check if nums[j] < nums[i]. If this condition is true, we calculate the maximum value in the LIS table for jth index and add 1 to it (to include the current element).

We then update the LIS value in the lis[i] position, and if this value is greater than the current maxLength, we update maxLength with this value.

Finally, we return the maxLength as the result of our LIS calculation.

The runtime complexity of the dynamic programming solution for the LIS problem is $O(n^2)$ since we need to loop over all previous indexes for each index in the input array. However, this is much more efficient than the exponential time complexity of the recursive approach. There is also a more advanced $O(nlogn)$ solution to the LIS problem that uses binary search, but this is beyond the scope of this answer.

2.18   Solve the Matrix Chain Multiplication problem using dynamic programming.

The Matrix Chain Multiplication problem is a classic example of a dynamic programming problem. The problem is to determine the optimal order for multiplying a chain of matrices such that the total number of multiplications is minimized.

Suppose we have n matrices, and the dimensions of the i-th

matrix are represented by a pair of numbers (a_i, b_i), such that matrix i has dimensions a_i b_i. For simplicity, we can assume that all matrices are compatible for multiplication, that is, b_i-1 = a_i for i = 2, 3, ..., n.

The problem is to find the optimal order to multiply the matrices such that the total number of scalar multiplications is minimized. The number of scalar multiplications required to multiply two matrices of dimensions a b and b c is a b c.

We can use dynamic programming to solve this problem by breaking it down into subproblems and computing the solution to each subproblem only once.

Let's define the following variables:

```
- m[i,j], the minimum number of scalar multiplications needed to
      compute the product of matrices A[i]A[i+1]...A[j]
- s[i,j], the index of the matrix that should be used as the last in
      the multiplication of matrices A[i]A[i+1]...A[j]
```

The base case for our subproblem is when i == j, which means we have only one matrix, so m[i,i] = 0. For the general case, we can express m[i,j] recursively in terms of the subproblems as follows:

```
m[i,j] = min(m[i,k] + m[k+1,j] + A[i].row * A[k].col * A[j].col)
      for i  k < j
```

Where A[i].row and A[k].col represent respectively the number of rows of matrix Ai and the number of columns of matrix Ak. A[k].col represents the number of columns of matrix Aj.

The variable s[i,j] represents the index of the matrix that should be used as the last in the multiplication of matrices A[i]A[i+1]...A[j]. We can compute this variable as follows:

```
s[i,j] = argmin(m[i,k] + m[k+1,j] + A[i].row * A[k].col * A[j].
col) for i   k < j
```

Once we have computed m and s for every subproblem, we can then use the s table to construct the optimal order for multiplying the matrices.

Here's a Java implementation of the algorithm:

```java
public static int[] matrixChainOrder(int[] p) {
    int n = p.length - 1; // number of matrices
    int[][] m = new int[n][n]; // minimum scalar multiplications
    int[][] s = new int[n][n]; // matrix indexes

    // base case: single matrix
    for (int i = 0; i < n; i++) {
        m[i][i] = 0;
    }

    // compute minimum scalar multiplications
    for (int len = 2; len <= n; len++) {
        for (int i = 0; i < n - len + 1; i++) {
            int j = i + len - 1;
            m[i][j] = Integer.MAX_VALUE;
            for (int k = i; k < j; k++) {
                int q = m[i][k] + m[k+1][j] + p[i]*p[k+1]*p[j+1];
                if (q < m[i][j]) {
                    m[i][j] = q;
                    s[i][j] = k;
                }
            }
        }
    }

    // construct optimal order
    int[] order = new int[n];
    int index = 0;
    int i = 0, j = n - 1;
    while (i < j) {
        order[index++] = s[i][j];
        if (s[i][j] >= i+1) {
            order[index++] = s[i][j]-1;
        }
        i = s[i][j] + 1;
    }
    order[index] = n-2;

    return order;
}
```

The function 'matrixChainOrder' takes an array 'p' that represents the dimensions of the matrices, and returns an array 'order' that represents the optimal order for multiplying the matrices.

For example, if we have 4 matrices with dimensions 10x20, 20x30, 30x40, and 40x30, we can call 'matrixChainOrder' as follows:

```
int[] p = {10, 20, 30, 40, 30};
int[] order = matrixChainOrder(p);
System.out.println(Arrays.toString(order));
```

This would output the following:

```
[1, 2, 3, 0, 2]
```

This means that the optimal order for multiplying the matrices is A1 * A2 * A3 * A0 * A2, where Ai represents the matrix with dimensions 'p[i] x p[i+1]'.

2.19 Explain how the Traveling Salesman Problem (TSP) can be solved using dynamic programming.

The Traveling Salesman Problem (TSP) is a classic optimization problem that aims to find the shortest possible path that visits all given cities and returns to the starting city. The problem is considered as NP-hard and there is no known exact algorithm that solves it efficiently for all instances. However, dynamic programming can be used to solve TSP for relatively small instances.

The basic idea of using dynamic programming for TSP is to
break down the problem into sub-problems and solve them
recursively. Specifically, we can frame TSP as a problem of
finding the shortest path that visits a subset of cities and ends
at a specific city. Let's consider the following example,

City A is the starting city, and we want to find the shortest route that visits all six cities and returns to A. To apply
dynamic programming to this problem, we can define the subproblems and use their solutions to solve the original problem.
The sub-problems can be defined as follows:

For each city i and subset S of cities that includes city A and
i,

let dist(i, S) be the length of the shortest path that starts at
A, visits each city in S exactly once, and ends at i.

Using this definition, we can write a recursive formula for dist(i,
S) in terms of smaller sub-problems:

```
dist(i, {A, i}) = distance(A, i)
dist(i, S) = min { distance(j, i) + dist(j, S - {i}) } for all j in S
    except A and i.
```

Here, distance(j, i) is the distance between cities j and i, and
S - i denotes the set obtained by removing city i from the set
S.

Intuitively, the recursive formula computes the length of the
shortest path that starts at A, visits each city in S exactly
once, and ends at i, by considering all possible ways of arriving
at i from some city j in S, visiting the remaining cities in S - i
in the shortest possible way, and then continuing to i.

Once we have computed all dist(i, S) for all i and all subsets

S that include A and i, we can find the optimal TSP path of
length L* by finding the minimum of (distance(i, A) + dist(i,
S - i)) for each i, where S is the set of all cities except A and i.

Here is the code to solve TSP problem using dynamic programming:

```java
public class TravelingSalesmanProblem {
    private static final int INF = 9999999;
    private int n;
    private int[][] distance;
    private int[][] memo;

    public TravelingSalesmanProblem(int[][] distance) {
        this.distance = distance;
        this.n = distance.length;
        memo = new int[n][1 << n];
    }

    public int solve() {
        for (int i = 0; i < n; i++) {
            Arrays.fill(memo[i], -1);
        }
        return tsp(0, 1);
    }

    private int tsp(int current, int visited) {
        if (visited == (1 << n) - 1) {
            return distance[current][0];
        }
        if (memo[current][visited] != -1) {
            return memo[current][visited];
        }
        int minDistance = INF;
        for (int i = 0; i < n; i++) {
            if (i != current && ((visited & (1 << i)) == 0)) {
                int newDistance = distance[current][i] + tsp(i,
    visited | (1 << i));
                minDistance = Math.min(minDistance, newDistance);
            }
        }
        memo[current][visited] = minDistance;
        return minDistance;
    }
}
```

In this implementation, 'distance' is a 2D array that stores
the distances between all pairs of cities, and 'n' is the number

of cities. The 'memo' array is used to store the solutions of sub-problems to avoid recomputation. The 'solve' method initializes the 'memo' array and calls the recursive 'tsp' method with the starting city (0) and the bit representation of the set of visited cities (initially only the starting city is visited). The 'tsp' method recursively computes the length of the shortest path that starts at the current city, visits all unvisited cities and returns to the starting city. The computation is based on the recursive formula described above. Finally, the method returns the computed length.

Overall, dynamic programming allows us to solve TSP in $O(n^2 * 2^n)$ time complexity, where n is the number of cities. Although this is not an efficient solution for large values of n, it helps us understand the problem and provides a baseline for developing more efficient algorithms.

2.20 Solve the problem of finding the Longest Palindromic Subsequence (LPS) using dynamic programming.

The Longest Palindromic Subsequence (LPS) problem is defined as finding the longest subsequence (not necessarily contiguous) of a given string that is a palindrome.

There are several ways to solve the LPS problem, but we can use dynamic programming to find an efficient solution. The idea is to build a table where each cell (i, j) represents the length of the LPS for the subsequence of the string s starting at i and ending at j. We can fill this table using a bottom-up approach.

Let's define the function 'lps(s)' that takes a string 's' as input
and returns the length of its LPS. Here's the dynamic programming algorithm to calculate it:

```java
public int lps(String s) {
    int n = s.length(); // length of the string

    /* Create the table to store the LPS lengths */
    int[][] table = new int[n][n];

    /* Strings of length 1 have LPS of length 1 */
    for (int i = 0; i < n; i++) {
        table[i][i] = 1;
    }

    /* Build the table bottom-up */
    for (int len = 2; len <= n; len++) {
        for (int i = 0; i < n - len + 1; i++) {
            int j = i + len - 1;
            if (s.charAt(i) == s.charAt(j) && len == 2) {
                table[i][j] = 2;
            } else if (s.charAt(i) == s.charAt(j)) {
                table[i][j] = table[i + 1][j - 1] + 2;
            } else {
                table[i][j] = Math.max(table[i + 1][j], table[i][j -
1]);
            }
        }
    }

    /* Return the length of the LPS */
    return table[0][n - 1];
}
```

Let's walk through the algorithm step by step and see how it
works.

First, we create a 2D array 'table' of size n x n to store the LPS
lengths for all substrings. We initialize the diagonal cells (i.e.,
substrings of length 1) with 1, because any single character is
always a palindrome of length 1.

Next, we fill the remaining cells of 'table' iteratively. We start
with substrings of length 2 and increment the length of the substring by 1 in each iteration until we reach the whole string.

For each substring, we compare the first and last characters. If they are the same, the LPS length is the LPS length of the substring without the first and last characters, plus 2 (because we add the first and last characters to form a longer palindrome). If they are not the same, we take the maximum of the LPS length of the substring without the first character and the LPS length of the substring without the last character.

Finally, we return the LPS length of the whole string, which is stored in 'table[0][n-1]'.

Let's see an example. Suppose we want to find the LPS of the string "ABBDCACB". Here's how the 'table' would be filled:

```
    A   B   B   D   C   A   C   B
A   1   1   1   1   1   1   1   1
B       1   2   2   2   2   2   3
B           1   1   1   1   1   1
D               1   1   1   1   1
C                   1   1   1   1
A                       1   1   1
C                           1   1
B                               1
```

The LPS of "ABBDCACB" is "BCACB", which has length 5.

The time complexity of this algorithm is $O(n^2)$ because we fill a n x n table. The space complexity is also $O(n^2)$ because we use a n x n table to store the LPS lengths. However, we can improve the space complexity to $O(n)$ by using a 1D array instead of a 2D array to store the LPS lengths of the current and previous substrings. This can be achieved by using a "rolling" array technique or by swapping two arrays alternately.

Chapter 3

Intermediate

3.1 Explain the concept of state space reduction and how it applies to dynamic programming problems.

State space reduction is a technique used in dynamic programming to reduce the number of possible states that need to be considered in order to solve a problem. This is done by identifying and eliminating states that are either unnecessary or redundant. This reduces the complexity of the problem and improves the efficiency of the algorithm.

There are two ways to achieve state space reduction: 1) memoization, and 2) tabulation.

1. Memoization: Memoization involves storing the values of subproblems that have already been solved in a table or cache.

This enables the algorithm to avoid recomputing the same sub-problem multiple times. By storing the values of subproblems that have already been solved, we can avoid computing them again, greatly reducing the state space of the problem. Memoization works well when the problem can be broken into smaller subproblems that can be easily solved, such as in the Fibonacci sequence, where each subproblem is to compute the sum of two smaller Fibonacci numbers.

Here is an example of applying memoization to compute the factorial of a number:

```
public static int factorial(int n, int[] memo) {
    if (n <= 1) {
        return 1;
    } else if (memo[n] != 0) {
        return memo[n];
    } else {
        int result = n * factorial(n - 1, memo);
        memo[n] = result;
        return result;
    }
}
```

2. Tabulation: Tabulation involves building a table of solutions to smaller subproblems and using them to solve larger subproblems. This technique involves filling up a table with the solutions to the subproblems in a specific order. This order is usually the order in which the subproblems can be solved recursively. This technique is generally used when the subproblems are of fixed size and can be indexed in a table. By building up the solutions to the subproblems in a table, we can reduce the state space required to solve the larger problem.

Here is an example of applying tabulation to find the minimum number of coins required to make change for a given amount:

```
public static int minCoins(int[] coins, int amount) {
    int[] table = new int[amount + 1];
```

```java
    for (int i = 1; i <= amount; i++) {
        table[i] = Integer.MAX_VALUE;
    }
    table[0] = 0;
    for (int i = 1; i <= amount; i++) {
        for (int j = 0; j < coins.length; j++) {
            if (coins[j] <= i) {
                int subResult = table[i - coins[j]];
                if (subResult != Integer.MAX_VALUE && subResult + 1 <
    table[i]) {
                    table[i] = subResult + 1;
                }
            }
        }
    }
    return table[amount];
}
```

In conclusion, state space reduction is an important concept in dynamic programming that reduces the complexity of the problem by identifying and eliminating unnecessary or redundant states. This greatly improves the efficiency of the algorithm, and is achieved through techniques such as memoization and tabulation.

3.2 How can you use dynamic programming to solve the Edit Distance problem? Implement the solution.

The Edit Distance problem involves finding the minimum number of edits (insertion, deletion, or substitution) needed to transform one string into another. This problem can be solved using dynamic programming.

The dynamic programming approach for the Edit Distance problem involves building a table that stores the minimum number of edits required to transform prefixes of the two strings being compared. We build up the solution for larger prefixes by using solutions to smaller prefixes.

Let's consider an example where we want to transform the word "kitten" to "sitting". We can solve this problem using dynamic programming as follows:

1. We create a table with (m+1) rows and (n+1) columns where m and n are the lengths of the two strings being compared. In our case, the table will have 7 rows and 7 columns.

2. We fill the first row and column of the table with values representing the number of edits needed to transform an empty string to the corresponding prefix of the other string. For example, the first row will be filled with values 0, 1, 2, 3, 4, 5, 6 as we need 0, 1, 2, 3, 4, 5, and 6 edits to convert an empty string to the prefix of the string "sitting" of length 0, 1, 2, 3, 4, 5, and 6.

3. We fill the rest of the table using the following recurrence relation:

```
if word1[i-1] == word2[j-1]:
    dp[i][j] = dp[i-1][j-1]
else:
    dp[i][j] = min(dp[i-1][j], dp[i][j-1], dp[i-1][j-1]) + 1
```

The above code compares each character of both strings and calculates the minimum cost by:

```
- 1 gap insertion = dp[i-1][j]+1
- 1 gap deletion  = dp[i][j-1]+1
- 1 substitution = dp[i-1][j-1]+1
```

4. The final value present in the bottom right-most cell of the table represents the minimum number of edits required to transform the first string to the second string.

Heres the Java implementation of the algorithm:

```java
public static int editDistance(String word1, String word2) {
    int m = word1.length();
    int n = word2.length();

    int[][] dp = new int[m+1][n+1];

    // fill the first row and column of the table
    for(int i=0; i<=m; i++) {
        dp[i][0] = i;
    }

    for(int i=0; i<=n; i++) {
        dp[0][i] = i;
    }

    // fill the rest of the table
    for(int i=1; i<=m; i++) {
        for(int j=1; j<=n; j++) {
            if(word1.charAt(i-1) == word2.charAt(j-1)) {
                dp[i][j] = dp[i-1][j-1];
            } else {
                dp[i][j] = Math.min(dp[i-1][j], Math.min(dp[i][j-1],
    dp[i-1][j-1])) + 1;
            }
        }
    }

    // return the final value in the table
    return dp[m][n];
}
```

Let's test the algorithm with the example we used earlier:

```java
String word1 = "kitten";
String word2 = "sitting";
int result = editDistance(word1, word2);

System.out.println(result); // output: 3
```

The output is 3 which means it will take 3 edits to transform "kitten" to "sitting".

3.3   Implement the Rod Cutting problem using dynamic programming.

The Rod Cutting problem is a classic optimization problem in which we are given a rod of length N and a price list that contains the prices of all possible rod lengths up to N. Our task is to cut the rod into smaller pieces in such a way that we can maximize our profit.

Here's an optimal substructure for the problem: suppose we know the optimal solution for a rod of length k, then we can easily compute the optimal solution for a rod of length N (N > k) by just considering every possible cut of length k and adding the price of that cut with the optimal solution for a rod of length (N-k).

Let's use dynamic programming to solve the problem step by step:

1. Define the problem in terms of smaller subproblems:

For a given rod of length i, let's say we are given an array 'price' where price[j] represents the price for a rod of length j. We want to find the maximum revenue we can obtain by cutting up the rod and selling the pieces.

2. Define the optimal value function:

Let's define R[i] as the maximum revenue we can obtain by cutting a rod of length i. Our task is to calculate R[N], which is the maximum revenue we can obtain by cutting a rod of length N.

3. Define the base case:

We want to start with a rod of length 0, so R[0] = 0.

4. Define the recursive function:

We can calculate R[i] for all values of i in the following way:

```
int[] price = {0, 1, 5, 8, 9, 10, 17, 17, 20};

int rodCutting(int N, int[] price) {
    int[] R = new int[N+1];
    R[0] = 0;

    for(int i=1; i<=N; i++) {
        int maxVal = Integer.MIN_VALUE;
        for(int j=1; j<=i; j++) {
            maxVal = Math.max(maxVal, price[j]+R[i-j]);
        }
        R[i] = maxVal;
    }

    return R[N];
}

System.out.println(rodCutting(8, price)); // Output: 22
```

In the above code, we are iterating through all possible cut lengths j for a rod of length i and calculating the maximum revenue we can obtain by using the optimal solution for a rod of length (i-j) and adding the revenue obtained by cutting a rod of length j.

5. Define the solution:

The solution to the problem is stored in R[N], which is the maximum revenue we can obtain by cutting a rod of length N.

In the above example, the optimal solution for a rod of length 8 is obtained by cutting it into two pieces of length 2 and 6, which gives us a revenue of 1+17 = 18 for the first piece and a revenue of 17+5 = 22 for the second. Therefore, the maximum revenue we can obtain is 22.

3.4 Discuss the trade-offs between top-down and bottom-up dynamic programming approaches in terms of time and space complexity.

Top-down and bottom-up are two common approaches for implementing dynamic programming algorithms.

Top-down dynamic programming, also known as memoization, involves starting with the original problem and recursively breaking it down into smaller subproblems until reaching the base case(s), and storing the solutions to the subproblems in a data structure, such as a hashmap or an array. When the solution to the original problem is needed, it is retrieved from the data structure instead of re-solving it.

Bottom-up dynamic programming, also known as tabulation, involves building the solution to the original problem by iteratively solving the subproblems in a bottom-up manner. This means that we start with the base case(s) and solve the subproblems iteratively, storing the solution of each subproblem in an array or table. Finally, we return the solution to the original problem, which is usually the last entry in the table.

The trade-offs between the two approaches are as follows:

1. Time complexity: Generally, top-down dynamic programming has a higher time complexity than bottom-up dynamic programming. This is because the top-down approach can result in solving subproblems multiple times. In contrast, bottom-up dynamic programming solves each subproblem just once and then uses already-computed results to solve larger sub-

problems. The time complexity of top-down dynamic programming can be improved by adding memoization, which stores the solution to a subproblem in a data structure when it is first computed and uses it later instead of solving the same subproblem again.

2. Space complexity: The space complexity of the two approaches can vary depending on the specific problem. In general, top-down dynamic programming is more memory-efficient than bottom-up dynamic programming because it only stores the results of the subproblems that are needed. On the other hand, bottom-up dynamic programming stores all the results of the subproblems in a table. However, in some problems, the top-down approach has higher space complexity due to the recursive calls, which can result in a large call stack.

Consider the example of the Fibonacci sequence. To compute the nth number in the Fibonacci sequence, we can use dynamic programming. The top-down approach would look like this in Java:

```java
public int fibonacciTopDown(int n, int[] memo) {
    if (memo[n] != 0) {
        return memo[n];
    }
    if (n == 1 || n == 2) {
        return 1;
    }
    memo[n] = fibonacciTopDown(n - 1, memo) + fibonacciTopDown(n - 2,
      memo);
    return memo[n];
}
```

In the above code, 'memo' is an array used for memoization. We check if the nth Fibonacci number has already been computed and stored in the array. If it has, we retrieve it from the array, otherwise we compute it recursively and store it in the array for later use.

The corresponding iterative bottom-up approach (tabulation) would look like this:

```
public int fibonacciBottomUp(int n) {
    if (n == 1 || n == 2) {
        return 1;
    }
    int[] dp = new int[n + 1];
    dp[1] = 1;
    dp[2] = 1;
    for (int i = 3; i <= n; i++) {
        dp[i] = dp[i - 1] + dp[i - 2];
    }
    return dp[n];
}
```

The 'dp' array stores the solutions to previously solved subproblems. We start with the base cases and fill in the table iteratively until we solve the original problem.

In terms of time complexity, both approaches have a time complexity of $O(n)$ because we need to solve each subproblem once. However, the top-down approach has a higher constant factor due to the recursive calls. In terms of space complexity, the bottom-up approach uses more memory because we need to store the solutions to all the subproblems in the 'dp' array.

In summary, the choice between top-down and bottom-up dynamic programming approaches depends on the specific problem and its constraints. If memory is tight or there are many overlapping subproblems, the top-down approach with memoization may be preferred. Otherwise, the bottom-up approach with tabulation is often faster and more memory-efficient.

3.5 What is the relationship between divide and conquer algorithms and dynamic programming? Provide an example.

Divide and conquer algorithms and dynamic programming both employ similar techniques to solve complex problems, but they differ in how they combine the smaller subproblems.

Divide and conquer algorithm divides the larger problem into smaller subproblems, solves each subproblem independently and then combines the subproblems' solutions to solve the original problem. On the other hand, Dynamic programming divides the problem into overlapping subproblems and then solves each subproblem only once and stores the result for future use.

In contrast to divide and conquer algorithms, dynamic programming often use memoization (top-down) or building a table (bottom-up) to store the solutions of subproblems. This approach optimizes the complexity of the algorithm by eliminating the need to solve the same subproblems multiple times.

For example, let's consider the problem of finding the n-th Fibonacci number.

A divide and conquer algorithm for the Fibonacci problem could look like:

```
public static int fibonacci(int n) {
    if (n == 0) return 0;
    if (n == 1) return 1;
    return fibonacci(n - 1) + fibonacci(n - 2);
}
```

This algorithm recursively computes the n-th Fibonacci number by dividing the problem into two subproblems (n-1) and (n-2). However, as we can see, this algorithm will perform multiple calculations of the same subproblem which can be optimized with dynamic programming.

A dynamic programming approach to solving Fibonacci problem would look something like this:

```
public static int fibonacciDP(int n) {
    int[] memo = new int[n + 1];
    return fibonacciMemo(n, memo);
}

private static int fibonacciMemo(int n, int[] memo) {
    if (n == 0) return 0;
    if (n == 1) return 1;

    if (memo[n] != 0) {
        return memo[n];
    }

    memo[n] = fibonacciMemo(n - 1, memo) + fibonacciMemo(n - 2, memo)
    ;

    return memo[n];
}
```

This algorithm uses dynamic programming to optimize the time complexity of the algorithm. It avoids repeated computation of the same subproblem in the divide and conquer approach by storing the results in memoization table. This way, the algorithm can compute the n-th Fibonacci number in $O(n)$ time complexity rather than exponential time complexity $O(2^n)$ of the normal divide and conquer approach.

Therefore, while divide and conquer and dynamic programming approaches share similarities in that they both rely on solving smaller subproblems, dynamic programming tends to use memoization techniques or building tables to optimize subproblem solution storage and reuse.

3.6   Implement the solution to the Maximum Sum Increasing Subsequence problem using dynamic programming.

The Maximum Sum Increasing Subsequence (MSIS) problem is to find the maximum sum subsequence of a given sequence such that all elements of the subsequence are sorted in increasing order. This problem can be solved using dynamic programming.

Let's consider the following example sequence:

```
sequence = [1, 101, 2, 3, 100, 4, 5]
```

To solve this problem, we will use an array 'msis' of size 'n' where 'n' is the length of the sequence. The 'i'th index of 'msis' will store the maximum sum of increasing subsequence ending at 'i'.

We can start by initializing all elements of 'msis' to their corresponding values in the sequence, since each element can be considered as a subsequence in itself.

```
msis = [1, 101, 2, 3, 100, 4, 5]
```

We can then iterate through the array 'msis' starting from the second element, and for each 'i'th element, we can find the maximum sum of increasing subsequence ending at 'i' by iterating through all elements before 'i' and finding the maximum value of 'msis[j] + sequence[i]' where 'j' is less than 'i' and 'sequence[j]' is less than 'sequence[i]'.

```
for i in range(1, n):
    for j in range(i):
```

```
if sequence[j] < sequence[i]:
    msis[i] = max(msis[i], msis[j] + sequence[i])
```

After iterating through the entire array 'msis', the maximum sum of increasing subsequence in the original sequence can be found by finding the maximum element in the 'msis' array.

```
max_sum = max(msis)
```

The complete implementation of the MSIS problem in Java is as follows:

```java
public static int maxSumIncreasingSubsequence(int[] sequence) {
    int n = sequence.length;
    int[] msis = new int[n];
    for (int i = 0; i < n; i++) {
        msis[i] = sequence[i];
    }
    for (int i = 1; i < n; i++) {
        for (int j = 0; j < i; j++) {
            if (sequence[j] < sequence[i]) {
                msis[i] = Math.max(msis[i], msis[j] + sequence[i]);
            }
        }
    }
    int maxSum = Integer.MIN_VALUE;
    for (int i = 0; i < n; i++) {
        if (msis[i] > maxSum) {
            maxSum = msis[i];
        }
    }
    return maxSum;
}
```

For the example sequence '[1, 101, 2, 3, 100, 4, 5]', the maximum sum of increasing subsequence is '106' which can be obtained by the subsequence '[1, 2, 3, 100]'.

3.7 Solve the Word Break problem using dynamic programming.

The Word Break problem can be defined as follows: given a non-empty string 's' and a dictionary containing a list of non-empty words, determine if 's' can be segmented into a space-separated sequence of one or more dictionary words.

For example, given the string '"leetcode"' and the dictionary '["leet", "code"]', return true because '"leetcode"' can be segmented as '"leet code"'.

The dynamic programming approach to this problem involves breaking down the problem into smaller subproblems and solving them incrementally. We can use an array 'dp' of size 'n+1', where 'n' is the length of the input string, to keep track of whether a substring of 's' from index '0' to 'i-1' can be segmented into dictionary words. Initially all values in 'dp' are set to false.

We start by setting the first element of 'dp' to true since an empty string can always be segmented. We then iterate over the input string from left to right, and for each index 'i', we check whether there exists a j such that 'dp[j]' is true (meaning that the substring from index 0 to j-1 can be segmented) and the substring from index j to i-1 is a dictionary word. If such index j exists, we set 'dp[i]' to true.

Once we have iterated over the entire input string, the value of 'dp[n]' indicates whether the entire input string can be segmented into dictionary words. If 'dp[n]' is true, then the solution is yes, otherwise it is no.

Here is the Java code implementation of this approach:

```java
public boolean wordBreak(String s, List<String> wordDict) {
    int n = s.length();
    boolean[] dp = new boolean[n+1];
    dp[0] = true;

    for(int i=1; i<=n; i++){
        for(int j=0; j<i; j++){
            if(dp[j] && wordDict.contains(s.substring(j,i))){
                dp[i] = true;
                break;
            }
        }
    }

    return dp[n];
}
```

In this implementation, we iterate over all substrings 's.substring(j,i)' of the input string 's'. If the substring is found in the dictionary and there exists a previous index 'j' such that the substring from index '0' to 'j-1' can be segmented, we set 'dp[i]' to 'true'. By breaking out of the inner loop we avoid unnecessary iterations, as soon as we find that 'dp[i]' is true, we can break the j loop as there is no need to test other 'j' values.

Overall, the time complexity of this algorithm is $O(n^2)$, where n is the length of the input string, due to the nested loop over all substrings of 's'. The space complexity is also O(n), as we use an array of size 'n+1' to store the intermediate results of the dynamic programming algorithm.

3.8 Discuss the concept of optimal substructure in dynamic programming with an example.

Optimal substructure is a key concept in dynamic programming (DP) that describes the property of many problems where an optimal solution to the problem can be obtained by combining optimal solutions to its subproblems. It means that if we can solve the subproblems optimally, we can combine their solutions to solve the original problem optimally.

Let's take an example of the Fibonacci sequence to understand this concept better. The Fibonacci sequence is a series of numbers in which each number is the sum of the two preceding numbers. It can be represented by the following recursive formula:

```
Fib(n) = Fib(n-1) + Fib(n-2), for n>=2
Fib(0) = 0, Fib(1) = 1
```

To calculate 'Fib(n)', one way is to use recursion and compute 'Fib(n-1)' and 'Fib(n-2)' recursively to get the result. However, this approach can result in a lot of duplicate calculations, as the same subproblems may be solved multiple times.

Dynamic programming addresses this problem by breaking down the problem into smaller subproblems and solving each subproblem only once. The optimal substructure property of the Fibonacci sequence problem can be seen as follows,

* The optimal solution to 'Fib(n-1)' can be obtained by solving the subproblem, 'Fib(n-2)' and 'Fib(n-3)'

* The optimal solution to 'Fib(n-2)' can be obtained by solving the

subproblem, 'Fib(n-3)' and 'Fib(n-4)'

* ...

* The optimal solution to 'Fib(2)' can be obtained by solving the subproblem, 'Fib(1)' and 'Fib(0)'

Using this observation, we can avoid solving redundant subproblems and compute the value of the Fibonacci sequence using Dynamic Programming. Here's the DP solution of the above problem using memoization technique in Java,

```java
class Fibonacci{
    private int[] memo = new int[100];

    public int fib(int n){
        if (n == 0) return 0;
        if (n == 1) return 1;

        if (memo[n] != 0) {
            return memo[n];
        }

        int result = fib(n-1) + fib(n-2);

        memo[n] = result;

        return result;
    }
}
```

In this solution, we use an array 'memo' to avoid recomputing the same subproblems. This approach significantly reduces the time complexity of the algorithm.

Thus, the concept of optimal substructure in dynamic programming enables us to efficiently solve complex problems by breaking them down into smaller subproblems and computing optimal solutions to these subproblems.

3.9   Implement the solution to the Longest Common Increasing Subsequence (LCIS) problem using dynamic programming.

The Longest Common Increasing Subsequence (LCIS) problem asks us to find the length of the longest common subsequence of two given sequences such that the common subsequence is increasing.

Dynamic programming is a natural way to solve this problem. We can start by defining a 2D array 'dp' where 'dp[i][j]' represents the length of the LCIS of the first i elements of the first sequence and the first j elements of the second sequence.

To fill up the 'dp' array, we can use the following recurrence relation:

```
if seq1[i] == seq2[j]:
    dp[i][j] = 1 + max(dp[k][l]) where k < i and l < j
else:
    dp[i][j] = max(dp[i-1][j], dp[i][j-1])
```

The intuition behind this recurrence relation is as follows. If the ith element of the first sequence and jth element of the second sequence are equal, then the length of the LCIS will be the length of the LCIS up to the (i-1)th element of the first sequence and (j-1)th element of the second sequence plus one. We can calculate this value for all previous i and j and take the maximum to get the final value of 'dp[i][j]'.

If the ith element of the first sequence and jth element of the second sequence are not equal, then we need to consider two cases - either we include the ith element of the first sequence or the jth element of the second sequence in the LCIS. We take the

maximum of the length of the LCIS with and without including
the ith element and the length of the LCIS with and without
including the jth element to get the final value of 'dp[i][j]'.

The final answer would be the maximum value in the 'dp' array.

Here's the Java implementation of the LCIS problem:

```java
public static int LCIS(int[] seq1, int[] seq2) {
    int m = seq1.length, n = seq2.length;
    int[][] dp = new int[m+1][n+1];

    for (int i = 1; i <= m; i++) {
        for (int j = 1; j <= n; j++) {
            if (seq1[i-1] == seq2[j-1]) {
                int maxVal = 0;
                for (int k = 0; k < i-1; k++) {
                    for (int l = 0; l < j-1; l++) {
                        if (seq1[k] < seq1[i-1] && seq2[l] < seq2[j
-1]) {
                            maxVal = Math.max(maxVal, dp[k][l]);
                        }
                    }
                }
                dp[i][j] = 1 + maxVal;
            }
            else {
                dp[i][j] = Math.max(dp[i-1][j], dp[i][j-1]);
            }
        }
    }

    int ans = 0;
    for (int i = 1; i <= m; i++) {
        for (int j = 1; j <= n; j++) {
            ans = Math.max(ans, dp[i][j]);
        }
    }
    return ans;
}
```

In this implementation, we are iterating over all possible values
of 'i' and 'j' and filling up the 'dp' array. Then we iterate over
the entire 'dp' array again to find the maximum value, which
is the solution to the LCIS problem.

3.10 Solve the Egg Dropping Puzzle using dynamic programming.

The Egg Dropping Puzzle is a classic problem in dynamic programming, which aims to find the minimum number of trials required to determine the height at which an egg will break when dropped from a building. In this problem, we are given the number of eggs and the number of floors of a building, and we need to determine the minimum number of trials required to determine the exact floor from which the egg will break when dropped.

The brute force approach to solve this problem is to try dropping the egg from all the floors one by one, starting from the first floor and moving up, until the egg breaks. However, this approach can be very inefficient, especially for taller buildings.

To solve this problem efficiently using dynamic programming, we can break it down into smaller subproblems and use memoization to store the results of the subproblems to avoid redundant calculations.

Let's denote the number of eggs by 'n' and the number of floors by 'k'. We can define the state of the problem as '(n, k)', which means that we have 'n' eggs and 'k' floors remaining to consider. The goal is to find the minimum number of trials required to determine the exact floor from which the egg will break when dropped.

Let 'dp(n, k)' be the minimum number of trials required to determine the exact floor, given 'n' eggs and 'k' floors. At each floor 'i', we can either drop the egg or not drop the egg. If we drop the egg, then we need to consider the floors below 'i' (i.e., 'dp(n - 1, i - 1)'), since the egg will break if dropped from floor 'i'. If we don't drop the egg, then we need to consider the floors above 'i' (i.e., 'dp(n, k - i)'), since the egg will not break if dropped from floor 'i'.

Therefore, the optimal solution for 'dp(n, k)' can be computed as follows:

```java
public static int eggDrop(int n, int k) {
    int[][] dp = new int[n + 1][k + 1];

    // Base case 1: If there are no floors or only one floor, then we
    need one trial.
    for (int i = 1; i <= n; i++) {
        dp[i][0] = 0;
        dp[i][1] = 1;
    }

    // Base case 2: If there is only one egg, we need to try every
    floor one by one
    for (int j = 1; j <= k; j++) {
        dp[1][j] = j;
    }

    // Fill the rest of the table using the optimal substructure
    for (int i = 2; i <= n; i++) {
        for (int j = 2; j <= k; j++) {
            dp[i][j] = Integer.MAX_VALUE;
            for (int x = 1; x <= j; x++) {
                int maxDrops = 1 + Math.max(dp[i-1][x-1], dp[i][j-x])
    ;
                dp[i][j] = Math.min(dp[i][j], maxDrops);
            }
        }
    }

    return dp[n][k];
}
```

Let's break down the above code to understand it better.

First, we create a 2D array 'dp' of size '(n+1) x (k+1)' to store the minimum number of trials required for each state.

Next, we set the base cases. If there are no floors or only one floor, then we need one trial, regardless of the number of eggs we have. If we have only one egg, we need to try every floor one by one.

Then, we use the optimal substructure to compute the optimal solution for 'dp(n,k)'. For each egg 'i' and each floor 'j', we try dropping the egg from all the floors one by one, starting from the first floor and moving up, until the egg breaks. For each try, we compute the maximum number of trials required, taking into account the worst case scenario where the egg breaks or doesn't break. Finally, we choose the minimum number of trials required among all the floors for the current state.

After we have filled the entire table, the value in the last cell 'dp(n,k)' gives us the minimum number of trials required to determine the exact floor.

Overall, the time complexity of the above code is $O(nk^2)$, since we are filling up a 2D array of size '$(n+1)x(k+1)$' using nested loops. However, the space complexity can be reduced to $O(k)$ by using two 1D arrays, as we only need to store the previous and current rows of the table, not the entire table.

Example: Let's say we have 2 eggs and a building with 10 floors. The output will be '4', which means that the minimum number of trials required to determine the exact floor from which the egg will break when dropped is '4'. Here is an illustration of the optimal solution for this example:

10

9

8

7

6

5

4

3

2

1

We drop the first egg from the 4th floor, since it gives us the maximum coverage of floors (i.e., 4 floors below and 5 floors above). If the egg doesn't break, we then drop the second egg from floor 8, as we need to cover only the remaining floors above floor 4. If the first egg breaks, we drop the second egg from the 1st floor, since we need to cover only the remaining floors below floor 4.

3.11   Implement the solution to the Optimal Binary Search Tree problem using dynamic programming.

The Optimal Binary Search Tree (OBST) is a classic problem in dynamic programming, which is aimed at determining the optimal cost of searching for an element in a Binary Search Tree (BST).

Before diving into the DP solution, let's review some basic concepts related to BST:

- A BST is a binary tree where each node has a key greater than all the keys in the left sub-tree and less than all the keys in the right sub-tree.

- The keys of the BST are such that they will be accessed with some frequency. The more frequently accessed keys should be placed closer to the root of the tree to minimize the search cost.

- The search cost is the sum of the frequencies of all the keys that are accessed during a search.

So, given n keys and their frequencies, the task is to build a Binary Search Tree that has a minimal total search cost.

To solve this problem, we create a 2-D array 'C[i][j]' where '0 <= i, j <= n' representing the cost of the optimal BST containing keys 'k[i+1]' through 'k[j]' where 'k' is the array of keys sorted in increasing order. We also create a 2-D array 'W[i][j]' for the sum of the frequencies from 'k[i+1]' to 'k[j]'.

The base case is 'C[i][i] = W[i][i]' for all '0 i n'.

For i > j, 'C[i][j] = 0' as an empty tree has no cost.

For all i < j, the optimal cost is the minimum cost we can achieve by trying every possible root node in the BST of keys 'k[i+1]' to 'k[j]'. This optimal cost is given by the formula:

`C[i][j] = min(C[i][r-1] + C[r+1][j] + W[i][j])` where `i <= r <= j`

The above formula states that to compute the optimal cost for 'k[i+1]' to 'k[j]', we have to consider every possible 'r' as root node and recursively compute the optimal cost for left and right subtrees of 'r', then add the frequency of all nodes in 'k[i+1]' to 'k[j]', which gives 'W[i][j]'.

Once we have the above 2-D array 'C', 'C[0][n]' will give us the optimal cost of searching all elements in the BST.

Here's the Java code implementing the above algorithm:

```
public static int optimalSearchTree(int[] keys, int[] freq) {
    int n = keys.length;

    // create c[n+1][n+1] and w[n+1][n+1]
```

```java
int[][] c = new int[n+1][n+1];
int[][] w = new int[n+1][n+1];

// initialize the base case when i=j
for (int i = 0; i < n; i++) {
    c[i][i] = freq[i];
    w[i][i] = freq[i];
}

// fill in the tables diagonally
for (int l = 2; l <= n+1; l++) {
    for (int i = 0; i <= n-l+1; i++) {
        int j = i + l - 1;
        w[i][j] = w[i][j-1] + freq[j-1];
        c[i][j] = Integer.MAX_VALUE;

        // compute optimal cost for the subtree rooted at r
        for (int r = i; r <= j; r++) {
            int cost = ((r > i) ? c[i][r-1] : 0) +
                       ((r < j) ? c[r+1][j] : 0) +
                       w[i][j];
            if (cost < c[i][j])
                c[i][j] = cost;
        }
    }
}

return c[0][n-1];
}
```

The time complexity of the above code is $O(n^3)$ which is due to the three nested for-loops. However, since we only have to evaluate '$n * (n + 1)/2$' subproblems, the space complexity is $O(n^2)$.

3.12   How can you use dynamic programming to solve the Maximum Length Chain of Pairs problem? Implement the solution.

The Maximum Length Chain of Pairs problem can be solved using dynamic programming.

The problem is as follows: given an array of pairs (a1, b1), (a2, b2), ..., (an, bn), each pair (ai, bi) represents a directed edge from vertex ai to vertex bi, find the maximum length chain of pairs that can be formed. A chain of pairs is a sequence of pairs (ai, bi), (aj, bj), ..., (ak, bk) where (aj, bj) is directed from vertex ai to vertex aj.

The solution using dynamic programming involves sorting the array of pairs based on the second element (the b value) in increasing order. We then define an array dp where dp[i] represents the length of the longest chain that ends at pair i. We can then compute dp[i] by iterating over all pairs j where b[j] < a[i], and updating the value of dp[i] to max(dp[i], dp[j] + 1). The final answer is the maximum value in the dp array.

Here is the Java code for the solution:

```
public int findMaxChainLength(Pair[] pairs) {
    Arrays.sort(pairs, Comparator.comparingInt(pair -> pair.b));
    int[] dp = new int[pairs.length];
    Arrays.fill(dp, 1);
    for (int i = 1; i < pairs.length; i++) {
        for (int j = 0; j < i; j++) {
            if (pairs[j].b < pairs[i].a) {
                dp[i] = Math.max(dp[i], dp[j] + 1);
            }
        }
    }
    int maxLength = 0;
```

```
    for (int len : dp) {
        maxLength = Math.max(maxLength, len);
    }
    return maxLength;
}
```

In this code, we first sort the array of pairs based on the second element (b value). We then initialize the dp array with 1, since the length of a chain that consists of only one pair is always 1. We then iterate over all pairs i (starting from the second one) and all pairs j (before i), and update the value of dp[i] if b[j] < a[i]. Finally, we loop over the dp array and find the maximum value, which represents the length of the maximum length chain of pairs.

3.13   Solve the Longest Bitonic Subsequence problem using dynamic programming.

The Longest Bitonic Subsequence problem asks us to find the longest subsequence of an input sequence that first increases and then decreases.

Dynamic programming is a good fit for this problem since we can break it down into smaller subproblems and use the solutions to these subproblems to solve the overall problem.

We can approach this problem using two dynamic programming arrays - one to store the longest increasing subsequence ending at each index in the input sequence, and another to store the longest decreasing subsequence starting at each index in the input sequence.

Let's call the input sequence 'arr' of length 'n'. We can initialize both arrays to have a length of 'n' and all values to be 1, since the longest increasing/decreasing subsequence at any index will always be at least 1 (the element itself).

To compute the longest increasing subsequence for each index in 'arr', we can iterate through the array from left to right and compare the value at each index to all the values to its left. If 'arr[i] > arr[j]' (where 'j' is any index to the left of 'i'), we can update the longest increasing subsequence ending at 'arr[i]' to be the maximum value of 'lis[j] + 1' (the longest increasing subsequence ending at 'arr[j]' plus one for 'arr[i]' itself) and the current value of 'lis[i]'. Essentially, we are asking - if I include the element at index 'i', what is the longest increasing subsequence that I can form up to this point?

Similarly, to compute the longest decreasing subsequence for each index in 'arr', we can iterate through the array from right to left and compare the value at each index to all the values to its right. If 'arr[i] > arr[j]' (where 'j' is any index to the right of 'i'), we can update the longest decreasing subsequence starting at 'arr[i]' to be the maximum value of 'lds[j] + 1' (the longest decreasing subsequence starting at 'arr[j]' plus one for 'arr[i]' itself) and the current value of 'lds[i]'. Essentially, we are asking - if I include the element at index 'i', what is the longest decreasing subsequence that I can form starting from this point?

Finally, we can compute the longest bitonic subsequence by iterating through 'arr' and finding the maximum value of 'lis[i] + lds[i] - 1'. Note that we subtract one since we are double counting the value at index 'i'.

Here is the Java code implementation of the Longest Bitonic

Subsequence problem using dynamic programming:

```java
public static int longestBitonicSubsequence(int[] arr) {
    int n = arr.length;
    int[] lis = new int[n];
    int[] lds = new int[n];

    // initialize both arrays to have a length of n and all values to
    be 1
    Arrays.fill(lis, 1);
    Arrays.fill(lds, 1);

    // compute the longest increasing subsequence for each index in
    arr
    for (int i = 1; i < n; i++) {
        for (int j = 0; j < i; j++) {
            if (arr[i] > arr[j]) {
                lis[i] = Math.max(lis[i], lis[j] + 1);
            }
        }
    }

    // compute the longest decreasing subsequence for each index in
    arr
    for (int i = n - 2; i >= 0; i--) {
        for (int j = n - 1; j > i; j--) {
            if (arr[i] > arr[j]) {
                lds[i] = Math.max(lds[i], lds[j] + 1);
            }
        }
    }

    int maxBitonicLength = 0;
    // compute the longest bitonic subsequence by finding the maximum
    value of lis[i] + lds[i] - 1
    for (int i = 0; i < n; i++) {
        maxBitonicLength = Math.max(maxBitonicLength, lis[i] + lds[i]
    - 1);
    }

    return maxBitonicLength;
}
```

Let's say we have 'arr = 1, 11, 2, 10, 4, 5, 2, 1'. This sequence
has a longest bitonic subsequence of length 6, which is 1, 2,
10, 5, 2, 1. We can verify that this code returns the correct
answer:

```java
int[] arr = {1, 11, 2, 10, 4, 5, 2, 1};
int longestBitonicLength = longestBitonicSubsequence(arr);
```

```
System.out.println(longestBitonicLength); // Output: 6
```

3.14   Implement the solution to the Palindrome Partitioning problem using dynamic programming.

The Palindrome Partitioning problem can be stated as follows:

Given a string s, partition s such that every substring of the partition is a palindrome. Return all possible palindrome partitioning of s.

For example, given the string s = "aab", the possible palindrome partitionings are:

```
- ["aa", "b"]
- ["a", "a", "b"]
```

To solve this problem, we can use dynamic programming. We can use a 2D boolean array to store whether a substring from i to j is a palindrome. Then we can use backtracking to generate all possible palindrome partitionings.

Here's the Java code:

```java
public List<List<String>> partition(String s) {
    int n = s.length();
    boolean[][] isPalindrome = new boolean[n][n];

    // fill isPalindrome table
    for (int i = n - 1; i >= 0; i--) {
        for (int j = i; j < n; j++) {
            if (s.charAt(i) == s.charAt(j) && (j - i <= 2 ||
    isPalindrome[i + 1][j - 1])) {
                isPalindrome[i][j] = true;
            }
```

```
        }
    }

    List<List<String>> result = new ArrayList<>();
    dfs(result, new ArrayList<>(), s, isPalindrome, 0);
    return result;
}

private void dfs(List<List<String>> result, List<String> currentList,
    String s, boolean[][] isPalindrome, int start) {
    if (start == s.length()) {
        result.add(new ArrayList<>(currentList));
        return;
    }

    for (int end = start; end < s.length(); end++) {
        if (isPalindrome[start][end]) {
            currentList.add(s.substring(start, end + 1));
            dfs(result, currentList, s, isPalindrome, end + 1);
            currentList.remove(currentList.size() - 1);
        }
    }
}
```

The time complexity of this solution is $O(n^2)$ to fill the isPalindrome table, and the space complexity is also $O(n^2)$ to store the table. The backtracking part has a time complexity of $O(n * 2^n)$, since in the worst-case scenario, every substring is a palindrome and every partition is a single character, resulting in 2^n possible partitions. However, in practice, the number of possible partitions is much smaller than 2^n.

3.15   Explain how dynamic programming can be used to solve the Longest Repeated Subsequence problem.

The Longest Repeated Subsequence (LRS) problem is to find the longest subsequence that appears more than once in a given string. For example, in the string "ABAB", the longest repeated subsequence is "AB" because it appears twice.

Dynamic programming can be used to solve the LRS problem efficiently in $O(n^2)$, where n is the length of the string. The basic idea of dynamic programming is to break down the problem into smaller subproblems and solve each subproblem only once, storing the solutions in a table for later use.

We can define a 2D table dp[][] where dp[i][j] represents the length of the longest repeated subsequence of the first i characters of the string, considering the j characters. For example, if we have the string "ABCA", then dp[3][2] would represent the length of the longest repeated subsequence considering the first three characters "ABC" and the first two characters "AB".

To fill in the dp table, we can use the following recurrence relation:

If the i-th and j-th characters of the string are the same and i!=j:

```
dp[i][j] = dp[i-1][j-1] + 1
```

If the i-th and j-th characters of the string are not the same:

```
dp[i][j] = max(dp[i-1][j], dp[i][j-1])
```

The first case occurs when we find a character that matches a character that we have seen before. In this case, we can take the length of the longest repeated subsequence that we have found so far (dp[i-1][j-1]) and add 1 to it to include the matching character.

The second case occurs when we do not find a matching character. In this case, we take the maximum of the length of

the longest repeated subsequence considering the i-th character of the first string and the j-th character of the second string
(dp[i-1][j]) and the length of the longest repeated subsequence
considering the i-th character of the first string and the j-th-1
character of the second string (dp[i][j-1]).

The final answer to the LRS problem is the value in dp[n][n]
where n is the length of the string.

Here's the Java code for implementing the dynamic programming approach to solve the LRS problem:

```java
public static int lrs(String str) {
    int n = str.length();
    int[][] dp = new int[n+1][n+1];

    // Fill in the dp table
    for (int i = 1; i <= n; i++) {
        for (int j = 1; j <= n; j++) {
            if (str.charAt(i-1) == str.charAt(j-1) && i != j) {
                dp[i][j] = dp[i-1][j-1] + 1;
            } else {
                dp[i][j] = Math.max(dp[i-1][j], dp[i][j-1]);
            }
        }
    }

    return dp[n][n];
}
```

3.16   Solve the Minimum Cost Path prob-
lem in a grid using dynamic programming.

The Minimum Cost Path problem is a classic dynamic programming problem that involves finding the lowest cost path
from the top-left corner of a grid to the bottom-right corner,

while moving only down, right, and diagonally down-right.

To solve this problem using dynamic programming, we can create a grid of memoized values, where each cell represents the minimum cost to reach that cell from the top-left corner. We start by initializing the first row and first column with their cumulative values, since there is only one possible path to each cell in these lines.

Then, for each cell in the remaining part of the grid, we calculate the minimum cost to reach that cell by taking the minimum of the three neighboring cells: the cell above, the cell to the left, and the cell diagonally up and left. We add the cost of the current cell to the minimum of these three values to get the minimum cost path to that cell.

Finally, we return the memoized value in the bottom-right corner of the grid, which represents the minimum cost path to reach that point.

Here is an implementation of the Minimum Cost Path problem in Java:

```java
public static int minCostPath(int[][] grid) {
    int m = grid.length;
    int n = grid[0].length;
    int[][] memo = new int[m][n];

    // initialize first row and first column
    memo[0][0] = grid[0][0];
    for (int i = 1; i < m; i++) {
        memo[i][0] = memo[i-1][0] + grid[i][0];
    }
    for (int j = 1; j < n; j++) {
        memo[0][j] = memo[0][j-1] + grid[0][j];
    }

    // fill in rest of memoized grid
    for (int i = 1; i < m; i++) {
        for (int j = 1; j < n; j++) {
            memo[i][j] = grid[i][j] + Math.min(memo[i-1][j-1], Math.
```

```
    min(memo[i-1][j], memo[i][j-1]));
        }
    }

    // return bottom-right corner value
    return memo[m-1][n-1];
}
```

For example, if we have the following grid:

```
int[][] grid = {
    {1, 3, 5, 8},
    {4, 2, 1, 7},
    {4, 3, 2, 3}
};
```

The minimum cost path to reach the bottom-right corner is:

```
1 -> 3 -> 1 -> 2 -> 3
```

With a total cost of 8, which is returned by the 'minCostPath'
method.

3.17   Implement the solution to the Count All Possible Paths problem in a grid using dynamic programming.

The Count All Possible Paths problem in a grid is a classic
dynamic programming problem that asks to count all possible
paths from the top-left corner to the bottom-right corner of a
given grid.

One approach to solving this problem using dynamic programming is to build a two-dimensional array dp[][] to store the
number of paths to reach each cell of the grid. The approach

is to fill in this array row by row and column by column, where each value of dp[i][j] represents the number of paths to reach that cell from the top-left corner.

The base case for the array is when we can only move either right or down. In this case, there is only one way to reach any cell in the first row or first column. Thus, we can initialize the first row and first column of the array to 1.

After initialization, we can fill the rest of the array by summing up the number of paths to reach the current cell from the cell above it and the cell to the left of it, i.e., dp[i][j] = dp[i-1][j] + dp[i][j-1]. This is because we can only move either right or down.

Finally, the value of dp[m-1][n-1] represents the total number of paths from the top-left corner to the bottom-right corner of the grid.

Here's the Java implementation of the Count All Possible Paths problem in a grid using dynamic programming:

```java
public int countPaths(int m, int n) {
    int[][] dp = new int[m][n];

    // initialize first row to 1
    for (int i = 0; i < n; i++) {
        dp[0][i] = 1;
    }

    // initialize first column to 1
    for (int j = 0; j < m; j++) {
        dp[j][0] = 1;
    }

    // fill the rest of the array
    for (int i = 1; i < m; i++) {
        for (int j = 1; j < n; j++) {
            dp[i][j] = dp[i-1][j] + dp[i][j-1];
        }
    }
}
```

```
    // return the total number of paths
    return dp[m-1][n-1];
}
```

For example, if we call 'countPaths(3,3)', we get the output '6', which means there are 6 possible paths from the top-left corner to the bottom-right corner of a 3x3 grid. Here's a visualization of the grid and the paths:

```
1 1 1
1 2 3
1 3 6

Possible paths:
1. (0,0) -> (0,1) -> (0,2) -> (1,2) -> (2,2)
2. (0,0) -> (1,0) -> (2,0) -> (2,1) -> (2,2)
3. (0,0) -> (0,1) -> (1,1) -> (1,2) -> (2,2)
4. (0,0) -> (1,0) -> (1,1) -> (1,2) -> (2,2)
5. (0,0) -> (0,1) -> (1,1) -> (2,1) -> (2,2)
6. (0,0) -> (1,0) -> (2,0) -> (2,1) -> (2,2)
```

3.18   Solve the Subset Sum problem using dynamic programming.

The Subset Sum problem is a classic problem in computer science that involves finding whether a subset of integers in an array sum up to a given target sum. The problem is NP-complete, so we cannot solve it using a brute-force approach for large inputs. However, we can use dynamic programming to find an efficient solution.

The approach for solving the Subset Sum problem using dynamic programming involves creating a boolean matrix where each row represents an element from the array and each column represents a sum from 0 to the target sum. The value at each cell (i,j) in the matrix is true if it is possible to obtain the sum j using elements up to the ith position in the array, otherwise it is false.

To fill this matrix, we need to consider two cases:

1. If we exclude the ith element from the sum, we can see whether we can get the sum without the ith element, by looking at the value in the row above.

2. If we include the ith element in the sum, we can obtain the sum by adding the ith element to the sum (j-ith element), which is in the (i-1, j - arr[i]) cell.

After filling the matrix, we need to find a true value in the last row of the matrix, starting from the target sum. If such a value exists, it means that it is possible to obtain the sum using some elements from the array.

Here's the Java code implementation for solving the Subset Sum problem using dynamic programming:

```java
public static boolean subsetSum(int[] arr, int targetSum) {
    int n = arr.length;

    boolean[][] dp = new boolean[n+1][targetSum+1];

    for(int i=0; i<=n; i++) {
        dp[i][0] = true;
    }

    for(int i=1; i<=n; i++) {
        for(int j=1; j<=targetSum; j++) {
            if(arr[i-1] <= j) {
                dp[i][j] = dp[i-1][j-arr[i-1]] || dp[i-1][j];
            }
            else {
                dp[i][j] = dp[i-1][j];
            }
        }
    }

    return dp[n][targetSum];
}
```

Let's take an example to understand how this code works. Consider an array 3, 7, 4, 2 and target sum is 5. The boolean matrix after filling will look like:

```
i/j   0    1    2    3    4    5
0     T    F    F    F    F    F
1     T    F    F    T    F    F
2     T    F    F    T    F    F
3     T    F    T    T    T    T
4     T    F    T    T    T    T
```

As we can see, the value at dp[4][5] is true, which means it is possible to obtain the sum of 5 using elements from the array 3, 7, 4, 2.

Therefore, we have solved the Subset Sum problem using dynamic programming.

3.19   Implement the solution to the Maximum Product Cutting problem using dynamic programming.

The Maximum Product Cutting problem can be defined as follows: Given a rope of length n, what is the maximum product of lengths obtained by cutting the rope i.e. if the rope is cut into r pieces, then find the maximum product of lengths of r pieces.

The dynamic programming approach to this problem involves breaking down the problem into sub-problems and storing their solutions in a table, so that they can be referenced later when solving larger problems.

Let's define an array 'dp', where 'dp[i]' represents the maximum product that can be obtained from a rope of length 'i'. We will populate this array iteratively.

Our base cases are:

- 'dp[0] = 0'
- 'dp[1] = 0'

For a rope of length 'i', we iterate from 'j = 1' to 'j = i - 1', keeping track of the maximum product that can be obtained by cutting the rope at different positions. For each 'j', we calculate the current product as 'j * (i - j)' and add it to the maximum product that can be obtained from the remaining rope ('dp[i - j]').

The maximum of these products for different 'j' is stored in 'dp[i]'. This can be expressed as follows:

```
for(int i = 2; i <= n; i++){
    for(int j = 1; j < i; j++){
        dp[i] = Math.max(dp[i], j * (i - j) * dp[i - j]);
    }
}
```

Once the loop is complete, 'dp[n]' will contain the maximum product that can be obtained from the rope of length 'n'.

Here's the complete Java code for the solution:

```
public static int maxProductCut(int n) {
    int[] dp = new int[n + 1];
    dp[0] = 0;
    dp[1] = 0;
    for(int i = 2; i <= n; i++){
        for(int j = 1; j < i; j++){
            dp[i] = Math.max(dp[i], j * (i - j) * dp[i - j]);
        }
    }
    return dp[n];
}
```

Let's run a few test cases to verify our solution:

```
Input: n = 5
Output: 6
Explanation:
- Cut at 2, the product is maximum 2*3=6
- Cut at 3, the product is maximum 1*2*2=4
- Cut at 4, the product is maximum 3*1=3
Therefore, the maximum product is 6.

Input: n = 10
Output: 36
Explanation:
- Cut at 2, the product is maximum 2*8=16
- Cut at 3, the product is maximum 3*7=21
- Cut at 4, the product is maximum 4*6=24
- Cut at 5, the product is maximum 5*5=25
- Cut at 6, the product is maximum 3*3*4=36
- Cut at 7, the product is maximum 6*1*3=18
- Cut at 8, the product is maximum 2*6=12
Therefore, the maximum product is 36.
```

3.20   Solve the problem of finding the Minimum Number of Jumps to reach the end of an array using dynamic programming.

The problem of finding the minimum number of jumps to reach the end of an array is a classic dynamic programming problem. The problem statement is as follows: given an array of non-negative integers, where each element represents the maximum number of steps that can be taken forward from that element, find the minimum number of jumps to reach the end of the array.

One approach to solve this problem is to use dynamic programming. We can create an array 'dp' of the same length as the input array, where 'dp[i]' represents the minimum number of jumps needed to reach the end of the array starting from the

index 'i'. We can initialize 'dp[n-1]' to '0', as we can reach the
end from the end itself in 0 jumps. We can then iterate over
the rest of the array from right to left, and fill in the values of
'dp' as follows:

```
for(int i=n-2;i>=0;i--) {
    int jumps = Integer.MAX_VALUE;
    for(int j=1;j<=arr[i] && i+j<n;j++) {
        jumps = Math.min(jumps, dp[i+j]);
    }
    if(jumps != Integer.MAX_VALUE) {
        dp[i] = 1+jumps;
    }
}
```

In the above code, we iterate over all the possible jumps from
the current index 'i', and choose the one that results in the
minimum number of jumps required to reach the end. We then
add '1' to this value, as we are taking one jump to reach the
next index. We repeat this process for all the indices from right
to left, and finally return the value of 'dp[0]', which represents
the minimum number of jumps required to reach the end of
the array from the first index.

Let's take an example to understand this approach better.
Consider the following array:

```
arr = [2,3,1,1,4]
```

We start by initializing 'dp' as follows:

```
dp = [0,0,0,0,0]
```

We then iterate over the array from right to left. Starting from
the second last index, we have:

```
i=3, arr[i]=1
jumps = Integer.MAX_VALUE
dp[i+1] = 0
```

Since 'arr[i]=1', we can only take a jump of 1 from index 'i'. Therefore, we check the value of 'dp[i+1]', which is '0', and set 'jumps' to be '0'. We repeat this process for all the remaining indices, and finally obtain:

```
dp = [2, 2, 1, 1, 0]
```

The value of 'dp[0]' is '2', which is the minimum number of jumps required to reach the end of the array from the first index. Therefore, the answer to the problem is '2'.

Time Complexity: $O(N^2)$ where N is the length of the input array. In worst case, we may have to evaluate all the indices until the last index for each of the indices.

Space Complexity: O(N) where N is the length of the input array. We are using an additional array of the same length as the input array to store the minimum number of jumps from each index.

Chapter 4

Advanced

4.1 Implement the solution to the Box Stacking problem using dynamic programming.

The Box Stacking problem is a classic dynamic programming problem where given a set of boxes, the task is to find the maximum height that can be obtained by stacking the boxes on top of each other with the constraint that a box can only be placed on top of another box if its width and depth are smaller than the box below it.

We can solve this problem using dynamic programming in the following steps:

Step 1: Create an array of all possible rotations for each box. For example, if a box has dimensions (l, w, h), then all possible rotations can be (w,h,l), (h,l,w), (l,w,h).

Step 2: Sort the array of all boxes in descending order of the base area (width times depth).

Step 3: Create a new array dp[] where dp[i] stores the maximum height that can be achieved by using the ith box at the bottom of the stack. Initialize dp[] with the heights of each box.

Step 4: For each box i, check if it can be placed on top of another box j. If yes, then update dp[i] as dp[j] + height[i]. Also, keep track of the maximum height achieved so far.

Step 5: Return the maximum height achieved from dp[] array.

The Java implementation of the above steps is as follows:

```java
class Box implements Comparable<Box>{
    int l, w, h, area;
    Box(int l, int w, int h) {
        this.l = l;
        this.w = w;
        this.h = h;
        area = l*w;
    }
    public int compareTo(Box b) {
        return b.area - this.area;
    }
}

class BoxStacking {
    public int maxHeight(Box[] boxes) {
        int n = boxes.length;
        Box[] allBoxes = new Box[3*n];
        int index = 0;
        for(int i=0; i<n; i++) {
            Box box = boxes[i];
            allBoxes[index++] = new Box(box.l, box.w, box.h);
            allBoxes[index++] = new Box(box.w, box.h, box.l);
            allBoxes[index++] = new Box(box.h, box.l, box.w);
        }
        Arrays.sort(allBoxes);
        int[] dp = new int[3*n];
        for(int i=0; i<3*n; i++) {
```

```
        dp[i] = allBoxes[i].h;
    }
    int maxHeight = 0;
    for(int i=1; i<3*n; i++) {
        for(int j=0; j<i; j++) {
            if(allBoxes[i].l < allBoxes[j].l && allBoxes[i].w <
allBoxes[j].w) {
                dp[i] = Math.max(dp[i], allBoxes[i].h + dp[j]);
            }
        }
        maxHeight = Math.max(maxHeight, dp[i]);
    }
    return maxHeight;
    }
}
```

In the above implementation, the Box class represents each box with its dimensions and the compareTo method is used to sort the boxes in descending order of the base area. The maxHeight method takes an array of all boxes as input and returns the maximum height achieved.

We first create an array of all possible rotations for each box and sort them in descending order of the base area. We then initialize the dp[] array with the heights of each box.

We then iterate through each box i and check if it can be placed on top of another box j. If yes, then we update dp[i] as dp[j] + height[i]. We also keep track of the maximum height achieved so far. Finally, we return the maximum height from dp[] array.

The time complexity of the above implementation is $O(n^2)$ and the space complexity is $O(n)$.

4.2   How can you use dynamic programming to solve the Maximum Sum Rectangle problem in a 2D array? Implement the solution.

The Maximum Sum Rectangle problem is a classic problem in computer science where we have to find the sub-matrix with the maximum sum in a given 2D array. We can solve this problem using dynamic programming using an approach known as Kadane's algorithm.

Kadane's algorithm is used to solve the maximum sub-array problem in a 1D array. However, it can be extended to solve the maximum sub-matrix problem in a 2D array with a little modification.

The algorithm involves iterating over the 2D array row by row and keeping track of the maximum sum so far. For each row, we maintain a 1D array containing the sum of elements in the current row and all the previous rows up to the first row.

To compute the maximum sum rectangle, we will use two nested loops for the starting and ending row of the sub-matrix and keep track of the sum of elements in the sub-matrix. We then use Kadane's algorithm to find the maximum sum of elements in that sub-matrix and update the maximum sum found so far.

Here is the implementation of the dynamic programming solution to the Maximum Sum Rectangle problem in Java:

```
public static int maxSumRectangle(int[][] matrix) {
    int rows = matrix.length;
    int cols = matrix[0].length;
```

```
int maxSum = Integer.MIN_VALUE;

for (int i = 0; i < rows; i++) {
    int[] rowSum = new int[cols];
    // Add sum of all the rows above the current row
    for (int k = i; k < rows; k++) {
        int sum = 0;
        for (int j = 0; j < cols; j++) {
            rowSum[j] += matrix[k][j];
            sum += rowSum[j];
            maxSum = Math.max(maxSum, sum);
            // Use Kadane's algorithm to find the maximum sum of
    elements in the sub-matrix
            sum = Math.max(0, sum);
        }
    }
}
return maxSum;
}
```

In the above implementation, we first loop through all the rows of the matrix and maintain a 1D array 'rowSum' which contains the cumulative sum of elements in the 2D array up to the current row.

Then, we use two nested loops to consider all possible sub-matrices of the matrix and compute their sum. For each sub-matrix, we pass the 'rowSum' array to the Kadane's algorithm function, which returns the maximum sum of elements in the sub-matrix.

We keep track of the maximum sum found so far and return it once all the sub-matrices have been considered.

The time complexity of the above algorithm is $O(n^3)$, where n is the number of elements in the 2D array. However, it can be improved to $O(n^2$ by using the optimized Kadane's algorithm for 1D arrays.

4.3   Solve the Weighted Job Scheduling problem using dynamic programming.

The Weighted Job Scheduling problem is a common problem in computer science where we have N jobs, each with a start and end time, and a weight (profit) associated with completing the job. The objective is to find the maximum profit subset of mutually compatible jobs, where the jobs are compatible if they do not overlap in time.

We can solve this problem using dynamic programming by defining a subproblem and building a solution for the larger problem using the solutions to the subproblems. Let's write an algorithm and code in Java to solve this problem.

Algorithm:

1. Sort the jobs by their end times in non-decreasing order so that we can easily find the compatible jobs.

2. For each i ($0<=i<N$), let DP[i] be the maximum profit we can obtain by scheduling the jobs from 0 to i.

3. DP[0] = jobs[0].weight

4. For i from 1 to N-1, find the largest index j ($0<=j<i$) such that jobs[j] does not overlap with jobs[i] and set DP[i] = max(j, DP[j] + jobs[i].weight).

5. Return DP[N-1] as the maximum profit.

Code:

Here, we assume that we have a class "Job" with start and end times and weight attributes.

```
public int weightedJobScheduling(Job[] jobs) {
```

```
// Step 1: sort the jobs by their end times
Arrays.sort(jobs, (a, b) -> a.end - b.end);

// Step 2: define DP array
int N = jobs.length;
int[] DP = new int[N];

// Step 3: initialize DP[0]
DP[0] = jobs[0].weight;

// Step 4: fill DP array
for (int i = 1; i < N; i++) {
    DP[i] = jobs[i].weight;
    for (int j = 0; j < i; j++) {
        if (jobs[j].end <= jobs[i].start) {
            DP[i] = Math.max(DP[i], DP[j] + jobs[i].weight);
        }
    }
}

// Step 5: return DP[N-1]
return DP[N-1];
}
```

Example:

Suppose we have the following jobs:

```
| Job ID | Start Time | End Time | Weight |
|--------|------------|----------|--------|
|   J1   |     1      |    3     |   5    |
|   J2   |     2      |    5     |   6    |
|   J3   |     4      |    6     |   5    |
|   J4   |     6      |    7     |   4    |
|   J5   |     5      |    8     |   11   |
|   J6   |     7      |    9     |   2    |
```

Applying the algorithm in the previous code, we obtain DP = [5, 6, 6, 10, 16, 16]. The maximum profit is 16, which is obtained by selecting jobs J1, J2, and J5.

4.4 Implement the solution to the Optimal Strategy for a Game problem using dynamic programming.

The Optimal Strategy for a Game problem is a classic problem in dynamic programming. The problem statement is as follows:

Given an array of integers representing the values of coins in a game, two players take turns choosing a coin from one of the ends of the array until all coins have been chosen. The player with the highest sum of coins at the end wins. Assuming both players play optimally, write a function to determine the maximum amount of money the first player can win.

The optimal substructure of this problem is as follows: To calculate the maximum amount of money the first player can win, we need to determine the maximum amount of money the first player can win given the array A[i..j] (i and j are the indices of the beginning and end of the array). We can calculate this recursively by considering two cases:

1. The first player chooses A[i]: In this case, the second player can choose A[i+1] or A[j]. If the second player chooses A[i+1], then the first player must choose between A[i+2] and A[j]. If the second player chooses A[j], then the first player must choose between A[i+1] and A[j-1]. In both cases, the first player wins the value of A[i] plus the maximum amount of money the first player can win given the remaining array. This can be expressed as:

```
dp[i][j] = A[i] + min(dp[i+2][j], dp[i+1][j-1])
```

2. The first player chooses A[j]: In this case, the second player

can choose A[i] or A[j-1]. If the second player chooses A[i], then the first player must choose between A[i+1] and A[j-1]. If the second player chooses A[j-1], then the first player must choose between A[i] and A[j-2]. In both cases, the first player wins the value of A[j] plus the maximum amount of money the first player can win given the remaining array. This can be expressed as:

```
dp[i][j] = A[j] + min(dp[i+1][j-1], dp[i][j-2])
```

The base case is when i=j, in which case there is only one coin left, and the first player wins the value of that coin.

Using this recursive formula, we can construct the solution using dynamic programming. The time complexity of this DP solution is $O(n^2)$ and the space complexity is also $O(n^2)$. Here is the Java code that implements this DP solution:

```java
public static int optimalStrategy(int[] A) {

    int n = A.length;

    int[][] dp = new int[n][n];

    for (int i = 0; i < n; i++) {
        dp[i][i] = A[i];
    }

    for (int len = 2; len <= n; len++) {
        for (int i = 0; i < n - len + 1; i++) {
            int j = i + len - 1;
            if (A[i] >= A[j]) {
                dp[i][j] = A[i] + (i + 1 <= j - 1 ? Math.min(dp[i+2][
j], dp[i+1][j-1]) : 0);
            } else {
                dp[i][j] = A[j] + (i <= j - 2 ? Math.min(dp[i+1][j
-1], dp[i][j-2]) : 0);
            }
        }
    }

    return dp[0][n-1];
}
```

Let's test this function with an example:

```
int[] A = {3, 1, 7, 10};
int result = optimalStrategy(A);
System.out.println(result); // Output: 13
```

In this example, the optimal strategy for the first player is to choose the coin with value 3, then the coin with value 10. The second player can then only choose the coin with value 7. So, the first player wins $3 + 10 = 13$.

4.5 Discuss the concept of time and space complexity trade-offs in dynamic programming and how it can affect the choice of algorithm.

In dynamic programming, we often encounter problems where we can either solve them with a time complexity of $O(n^2)$ or $O(n)$ using either a top-down approach with memoization or a bottom-up tabulation approach. However, choosing between these two approaches will have an impact on both the time and space complexity of the algorithm.

In a top-down approach, we use memoization to store intermediate results to avoid unnecessary duplicate computations in recursive calls. This approach can have a high space complexity, as we need to store intermediate results in memory, and there can be a large number of recursive calls in the worst case. However, it can have a lower time complexity since we only compute the results we need and avoid the unnecessary calculations.

On the other hand, in a bottom-up approach, we use tabulation to pre-compute all intermediate results and fill them into a table or array. This approach can have a lower space complexity since we only need to store intermediate results once and not repeatedly in memory. It can also have a higher time complexity since we need to compute all the intermediate results and fill them in a table or array, even if they are not needed in the final result.

The choice of algorithm depends on the specific problem and its constraints. If we have limited memory space and a sufficiently fast computer, we may prefer to use the top-down approach to optimize for time complexity. If we have limited computing power and sufficient memory space, we may prefer to use the bottom-up approach to optimize for space complexity instead.

For example, let's consider the classic problem of finding the n-th Fibonacci number. A recursive implementation with memoization will have a time complexity of $O(n)$, as we only need to compute the results we need. However, it will have a space complexity of $O(n)$ since we need to store all the intermediate results in memory. A bottom-up implementation with tabulation will have a time complexity of $O(n)$, as we need to compute all intermediate results, including those we may not need. However, it will have a space complexity of $O(1)$, since we only need to store the last two Fibonacci numbers to compute the next one.

Overall, choosing between a top-down approach with memoization and a bottom-up approach with tabulation depends on the specific problem's characteristics and constraints, such as time complexity, space complexity, and speed of the computer. In practice, we often choose the approach that achieves the optimal balance between both factors.

4.6 Solve the Maximum Length of Pair Chain problem using dynamic programming.

The Maximum Length of Pair Chain problem is as follows:

You are given n pairs of numbers where each pair consists of two numbers. You are required to find the maximum length of pair chain. A pair (c, d) can follow another pair (a, b) if and only if b < c. So, you have to find the longest possible chain of these pairs such that pairwise second number of each pair is less than the first number of the next pair.

To solve this problem using dynamic programming, we need to define a subproblem and find the recurrence relation.

Subproblem: Given a pair (c, d), what is the length of the longest chain ending at (c, d)?

Let dp[i] represent the length of the longest chain ending at the i-th pair with $0 <= i < n$.

We can sort the pairs based on their first element in increasing order, i.e., pairs[i][0] < pairs[j][0] if i < j. This will allow us to only look at pairs that could come before a given pair in the chain.

Now, we can use bottom-up dynamic programming to solve the problem. We start by initializing dp[i] to 1 for all i.

For i in range [1, n), we look for all pairs j where j < i and pairs[j][1] < pairs[i][0]. Then we update dp[i] to max(dp[i], dp[j] + 1). This is because we can add the current pair after the longest chain ending at j to make a longer chain ending at i.

Finally, the answer is the maximum value in dp array.

Here is the Java code that implements the above dynamic programming approach:

```java
public int findLongestChain(int[][] pairs) {
    int n = pairs.length;
    Arrays.sort(pairs, (a, b) -> a[0] - b[0]); // sort based on first
        element
    int[] dp = new int[n];
    Arrays.fill(dp, 1);
    for (int i = 1; i < n; i++) {
        for (int j = 0; j < i; j++) {
            if (pairs[j][1] < pairs[i][0]) {
                dp[i] = Math.max(dp[i], dp[j] + 1);
            }
        }
    }
    int maxLen = 0;
    for (int len : dp) {
        maxLen = Math.max(maxLen, len);
    }
    return maxLen;
}
```

Let's run an example to see how it works:

```
Input pairs: [[1,2], [2,3], [3,4]]
Output: 2
```

Explanation: The longest chain is [1,2] -> [3,4] and its length is 2.

4.7   Implement the solution to the Assembly Line Scheduling problem using dynamic programming.

The Assembly Line Scheduling problem (also known as the Car Assembly problem) involves scheduling tasks at different stations along a production line. The goal is to minimize the total time taken to complete all tasks while ensuring that each task is completed on time and in the correct order. The problem is applicable in industries such as manufacturing, construction, and logistics.

We can solve the Assembly Line Scheduling problem using dynamic programming. The key idea behind dynamic programming is to break down a larger problem into smaller subproblems and store the solutions to these subproblems in a subproblem table to avoid redundant computations. Let us see the steps in detail -

1. Define the problem in terms of subproblems -

For the Assembly Line Scheduling problem, we can define the subproblems as follows -

Let's say we have 2 assembly lines, each with n stations.

$S_{i,j}$ represents the time taken to complete task j at station i.

$T_{i,j}$ represents the time taken to switch from station i to station i+1 on assembly line 1.

$U_{i,j}$ represents the time taken to switch from station i to station i+1 on assembly line 2.

E1 and E2 represent the entry times for the two assembly lines, respectively.

X1 and X2 represent the exit times for the two assembly lines, respectively.

Now, we can define the subproblems as follows -

f1(j) = Minimum time taken to complete all tasks on assembly line 1 up to station j.

f2(j) = Minimum time taken to complete all tasks on assembly line 2 up to station j.

2. Identify the base cases -

For the base case, we need to compute the time taken to complete the first task at each station on both assembly lines.

```
f1(1) = E1 + S1,1
f2(1) = E2 + S2,1
```

3. Define the recurrence relation -

The recurrence relation can be defined as -

```
f1(j) = min(f1(j-1) + Si,j, f2(j-1) + Ti,j + Si,j)
f2(j) = min(f2(j-1) + Si,j, f1(j-1) + Ui,j + Si,j)
```

The first line in the above equation calculates the time taken to complete task j on assembly line 1 by considering the minimum of two cases - 1. The time taken to complete task j-1 on assembly line 1 and then move to station j. 2. The time taken to complete task j-1 on assembly line 2, move from station j-1 to station j on assembly line 2, and then complete task j on assembly line 1.

Similarly, the second line in the above equation calculates the time taken to complete task j on assembly line 2.

4. Compute the final solution -

The total time taken to complete all tasks on both assembly lines is given by -

```
min(f1(n) + X1, f2(n) + X2)
```

The above equation calculates the minimum time taken to complete all tasks by considering the minimum of two cases - 1. The time taken to complete all tasks on assembly line 1 and then move to the exit. 2. The time taken to complete all tasks on assembly line 2 and then move to the exit.

With the above recurrence relation, we can solve the Assembly Line Scheduling problem using dynamic programming. Here is the Java code for the same -

```java
public class AssemblyLineScheduling {
    public static int assemblyLineScheduling(int[][] S, int[][] T,
    int[][] U, int[] E, int[] X) {
        int n = S[0].length;

        // Initialize base cases
        int f1 = E[0] + S[0][0];
        int f2 = E[1] + S[1][0];

        // Compute the optimal time for each station on both assembly
    lines
        for (int j = 1; j < n; j++) {
            int temp1 = f1;
            f1 = Math.min(f1 + S[0][j], f2 + T[1][j] + S[0][j]);
            f2 = Math.min(f2 + S[1][j], temp1 + U[0][j] + S[1][j]);
        }

        // Compute the final solution
        return Math.min(f1 + X[0], f2 + X[1]);
    }

    public static void main(String[] args) {
        int[][] S = {{4, 5, 3, 2},
                     {2, 10, 1, 4}};
        int[][] T = {{0, 7, 4, 5},
                     {0, 9, 2, 8}};
        int[][] U = {{0, 2, 3, 1},
                     {0, 2, 8, 9}};
```

```
    int[] E = {10, 12};
    int[] X = {18, 7};

    System.out.println("Optimal␣time:␣" + assemblyLineScheduling(
S, T, U, E, X));
    }
}
```

In the above example, we have two assembly lines with 4 stations each. We need to find the minimum time taken to complete all tasks on both assembly lines, given the time taken
to complete each task at each station and the switching times
between stations on both assembly lines. The entry and exit
times for both assembly lines are also given. The output of
the above program is 32, which is the minimum time taken to
complete all tasks.

4.8   How can dynamic programming be applied to solve the Longest Arithmetic Progression problem? Implement the solution.

The Longest Arithmetic Progression problem asks to find the
length of the longest subsequence of an array that forms an
arithmetic progression. For example, given the array '[3, 6, 9,
12]', the longest arithmetic progression is '[3, 6, 9, 12]' with a
length of 4.

Dynamic programming can be applied to solve this problem
using a bottom-up approach. We can define a 2D array 'dp[i][j]'
where 'dp[i][j]' represents the length of the longest arithmetic
progression that ends at indices 'i' and 'j' of the array.

To populate this array, we can iterate over each pair of indices '(i, j)' where 'j > i'. If the difference between 'arr[j]' and 'arr[i]' is the same as the difference between the previous pair of numbers in the arithmetic progression, then we can add 1 to 'dp[i][j]'. Otherwise, 'dp[i][j]' is initialized to 2 (since we have found two numbers in the arithmetic progression so far).

After populating the 'dp' array, we can find the maximum value in it and return it as the length of the longest arithmetic progression in the array.

Here is an example implementation in Java:

```java
public static int longestArithSeqLength(int[] arr) {
    int n = arr.length;
    int[][] dp = new int[n][n];
    int maxLength = 2;

    // Initialize dp array
    for (int i = 0; i < n; i++) {
        Arrays.fill(dp[i], 2);
    }

    // Populate dp array
    for (int j = 1; j < n; j++) {
        for (int i = 0; i < j; i++) {
            for (int k = 0; k < i; k++) {
                if (arr[i] - arr[k] == arr[j] - arr[i]) {
                    dp[i][j] = Math.max(dp[i][j], dp[k][i] + 1);
                    maxLength = Math.max(maxLength, dp[i][j]);
                }
            }
        }
    }

    return maxLength;
}
```

In this implementation, we iterate over each pair of indices '(i, j)' where 'j > i' and then iterate over all indices 'k' less than 'i'. If the difference between 'arr[j]' and 'arr[i]' is the same as the difference between 'arr[i]' and 'arr[k]', then we can update 'dp[i][j]' with the maximum length of the arithmetic progression ending at index 'i' and 'j'. Finally, we update 'maxLength' with the maximum value in the 'dp' array.

This implementation has a time complexity of $O(n^3)$ and a space complexity of $O(n^2)$. However, it can be optimized to have a time complexity of $O(n^2)$ using a hash table to store the index of each number in the array.

4.9 Solve the problem of finding the Largest Independent Set (LIS) in a binary tree using dynamic programming.

The Largest Independent Set (LIS) of a binary tree is defined as the largest subset of nodes in the tree such that no two nodes in the subset have an edge connecting them. In other words, the LIS is the largest set of nodes that can be selected from the tree in such a way that no two selected nodes are adjacent.

The dynamic programming approach to solve this problem involves recursively computing the LIS of each subtree of the binary tree, and then combining these results to obtain the LIS of the entire tree.

We can define a function LIS(node) which returns the size of the LIS of the subtree rooted at the given node. The function can be defined recursively as follows:

- If the given node is a leaf, the LIS is 1.

- If the given node is not selected, we can compute the LIS of its children and return the sum of these values.

- If the given node is selected, we cannot select any of its children.

Instead, we must compute the LIS of its grandchildren (the children of its children) and return the sum of these values plus one.

By using memoization (storing intermediate results), we can avoid recomputing the LIS of each subtree multiple times. The memoization table can be implemented using a HashMap, with the tree nodes as keys and the LIS values as values.

Here's a Java implementation of this approach:

```java
import java.util.*;

class TreeNode {
    int val;
    TreeNode left;
    TreeNode right;
    TreeNode(int x) { val = x; }
}

class LISBinaryTree {
    Map<TreeNode, Integer> memo = new HashMap<>();

    public int largestIndependentSet(TreeNode root) {
        if (root == null) return 0;
        if (memo.containsKey(root)) return memo.get(root);

        int size = 0;
        // compute LIS excluding root
        size += largestIndependentSet(root.left);
        size += largestIndependentSet(root.right);
        // compute LIS including root
        if (root.left != null) {
            size += largestIndependentSet(root.left.left);
            size += largestIndependentSet(root.left.right);
        }
        if (root.right != null) {
            size += largestIndependentSet(root.right.left);
            size += largestIndependentSet(root.right.right);
        }
        int lis = Math.max(size + 1, largestIndependentSet(root.left)
      + largestIndependentSet(root.right));
        memo.put(root, lis);
        return lis;
    }
}
```

We start by initializing a memoization table using a HashMap.

The 'largestIndependentSet' function takes a binary tree node as input, and recursively computes the LIS of the subtree rooted at that node using the memoization table to avoid re-computing values.

The size of the subtree LIS is computed by recursively calling 'largestIndependentSet' on the left and right child nodes, adding their return values, and adding the size of the LIS of the grandchildren of the root, if any. If the root is included in the LIS, we return the sum of the sizes of the grandchildren plus one. Otherwise, we return the maximum LIS excluding the root and the LIS including the root.

Finally, we look up the LIS of the root in the memoization table. If it is present, we return it. Otherwise, we add it to the memoization table and return it.

4.10 Implement the solution to the Minimum Partition problem using dynamic programming.

The Minimum Partition problem is a classic dynamic programming problem, where we are given an array of integers and we are asked to divide the array into two subsets such that the difference of the sum of the two subsets is minimized.

Let's assume that the input array is of length N and the sum of all elements in the array is sum. We need to find two subsets of the array S1 and S2 such that the absolute difference between the sum of S1 and the sum of S2 is minimized.

To solve this problem using dynamic programming, we can use a two-dimensional boolean matrix dp. The matrix dp[i][j] will be true if the sum j can be achieved using elements up to the i-th index in the input array.

The approach to filling this matrix is to start with the base case dp[0][0]=true (an empty set has a sum of zero) and dp[0][j]=false (cannot achieve any sum with an empty set, except zero), then for each element in the input array, we will either select it or not select it.

If the j-th value is less than or equal to the i-th element, we can either select it or not select it. If the j-th value is greater than the i-th element, we can not include i-th element in any subset if j-th value is less than i-th element.

So we fill the matrix as following:

```
dp[0][0] = true;
for (int i = 1; i <= N; i++) {
    for (int j = 0; j <= sum/2; j++) {
        dp[i][j] = dp[i-1][j];
        if (j >= arr[i-1]) {
            dp[i][j] |= dp[i-1][j-arr[i-1]];
        }
    }
}
```

Once we have calculated the dp matrix, the minimum difference between partition can be calculated by finding the largest value of j such that dp[N][j] is true. We can then calculate the difference between sum-j and j to find the minimum difference between the two subsets.

Here's the complete Java code implementation of the above algorithm:

```
public class MinimumPartition {
```

```java
public static int findMinimumPartition(int[] arr) {
    int N = arr.length;
    int sum = Arrays.stream(arr).sum();
    boolean[][] dp = new boolean[N+1][sum/2+1];

    // base cases
    dp[0][0] = true;
    for (int i = 1; i <= N; i++) {
        dp[i][0] = true;
    }

    // fill the dp matrix
    for (int i = 1; i <= N; i++) {
        for (int j = 1; j <= sum/2; j++) {
            dp[i][j] = dp[i-1][j];
            if (j >= arr[i-1]) {
                dp[i][j] |= dp[i-1][j-arr[i-1]];
            }
        }
    }

    // find the largest value of j such that dp[N][j] is true
    int j = sum/2;
    while (j >= 0 && !dp[N][j]) {
        j--;
    }

    // return the minimum difference
    return sum - 2*j;
}

public static void main(String[] args) {
    int[] arr = {1,6,11,5};
    int minDiff = findMinimumPartition(arr);
    System.out.println("The minimum difference between the two
subsets is: " + minDiff);
}
}
```

The output of the above code will be:

```
The minimum difference between the two subsets is: 1
```

In this example, the two subsets of the input array are 1,5 and 6,11. The difference between their sum is minimized to 1.

4.11   Solve the Wildcard Pattern Matching problem using dynamic programming.

The Wildcard Pattern Matching problem involves finding if a given string matches a pattern that contains special characters called wildcards. Wildcards can match any character in the string. There are two types of wildcards, '*' and '¿. The '*' wildcard matches zero or more characters, while the '¿ wildcard matches any single character.

For example, the pattern 'h*llo¿ matches the strings "hello", "hallo", "hxllol", and "hcllo?", but not "hllo" or "hellno".

To solve this problem using dynamic programming, we can define a 2D boolean array 'dp', where 'dp[i][j]' represents if the prefix of the string up to index 'i' matches the pattern up to index 'j'.

We can start by initializing 'dp[0][0]' to 'true', since an empty string matches an empty pattern. We can then fill in the first row of 'dp' to check if the pattern matches an empty string.

Next, we can iterate through the remaining cells in 'dp', using the following recurrence relation:

```
if (pattern.charAt(j - 1) == '*') {
    dp[i][j] = dp[i][j - 1] || dp[i - 1][j];
} else if (pattern.charAt(j - 1) == '?' || pattern.charAt(j - 1) ==
    str.charAt(i - 1)) {
    dp[i][j] = dp[i - 1][j - 1];
} else {
    dp[i][j] = false;
}
```

The first case handles the '*' wildcard. If the current character in the pattern is '*', we can either choose to ignore it (i.e. match zero characters), or match the current character in the string by setting 'dp[i][j]' to 'dp[i][j-1]' (ignore the wildcard) or 'dp[i-1][j]' (match the wildcard by adding a character to the string).

The second case handles the '¿ wildcard or a matching character. If the current character in the pattern is a '¿ or matches the current character in the string, we simply continue to match the remaining characters by setting 'dp[i][j]' to 'dp[i-1][j-1]'.

The third case covers any other scenario where the pattern and string do not match. In this case, we set 'dp[i][j]' to 'false'.

At the end of the iteration, 'dp[str.length()][pattern.length()]' will tell us if the entire string matches the entire pattern.

Here is the code implementation in Java:

```java
public static boolean isWildcardMatch(String str, String pattern) {
    boolean[][] dp = new boolean[str.length() + 1][pattern.length() +
        1];
    dp[0][0] = true;

    // Fill first row
    for (int j = 1; j <= pattern.length(); j++) {
        if (pattern.charAt(j - 1) == '*') {
            dp[0][j] = dp[0][j - 1];
        }
    }

    // Fill remaining cells
    for (int i = 1; i <= str.length(); i++) {
        for (int j = 1; j <= pattern.length(); j++) {
            if (pattern.charAt(j - 1) == '*') {
                dp[i][j] = dp[i][j - 1] || dp[i - 1][j];
            } else if (pattern.charAt(j - 1) == '?' || pattern.charAt
    (j - 1) == str.charAt(i - 1)) {
                dp[i][j] = dp[i - 1][j - 1];
            } else {
                dp[i][j] = false;
            }
        }
    }
```

```
    }
    return dp[str.length()][pattern.length()];
}
```

4.12   Implement the solution to the Distinct Subsequences problem using dynamic programming.

The Distinct Subsequences problem is as follows: given two strings 's' and 't', count the number of distinct subsequences of 't' in 's'.

We can solve this problem using dynamic programming. Let 'dp[i][j]' be the number of distinct subsequences of 't' in 's' up to index 'i' of 's' and up to index 'j' of 't'. If 's[i] == t[j]', then we can either include or exclude 's[i]' in the subsequence. If we include 's[i]', then the number of distinct subsequences is 'dp[i-1][j-1]'. If we exclude 's[i]', then the number of distinct subsequences is 'dp[i-1][j]'. If 's[i] != t[j]', then we can only exclude 's[i]' and the number of distinct subsequences is 'dp[i-1][j]'.

The base cases are 'dp[0][0] = 1' and 'dp[i][0] = 1' for all 'i', since there is only one way to form the empty subsequence. Also, 'dp[0][j] = 0' for all 'j > 0', since there are no subsequences of 't' in an empty string.

The final answer is 'dp[m][n]', where 'm' and 'n' are the lengths of 's' and 't', respectively.

Here is the Java code to implement the above approach:

```java
public int numDistinct(String s, String t) {
    int m = s.length();
    int n = t.length();
    int[][] dp = new int[m+1][n+1];

    // base cases
    for (int i = 0; i <= m; i++) {
        dp[i][0] = 1;
    }

    // fill dp table
    for (int i = 1; i <= m; i++) {
        for (int j = 1; j <= n; j++) {
            if (s.charAt(i-1) == t.charAt(j-1)) {
                dp[i][j] = dp[i-1][j-1] + dp[i-1][j];
            } else {
                dp[i][j] = dp[i-1][j];
            }
        }
    }

    return dp[m][n];
}
```

Let's go over an example to see how this works. Consider 's = "babgbag"' and 't = "bag"'. The dp table would look like:

```
      b   a   g
   0  1   0   0
b  1  1   0   0
a  1  1   1   0
b  2  1   1   0
g  3  1   1   1
b  3  4   1   1
a  3  4   5   1
g  3  4   5   6
```

The final answer is 'dp[7][3] = 6', which is the number of distinct subsequences of 't = "bag"' in 's = "babgbag"'.

4.13   Explain how dynamic programming can be used to solve the Maximum Sum Non-Adjacent Elements problem.

The Maximum Sum Non-Adjacent Elements problem requires finding the maximum sum that can be obtained by selecting a subset of non-adjacent elements from an array of positive integers. For example, given the array [1, 2, 3, 4, 5], the maximum sum non-adjacent elements are [1, 3, 5], with a total sum of 9.

Dynamic programming is a useful technique for solving this problem because it allows us to avoid redundant calculations and speed up the computation. We can use dynamic programming to build up a solution from smaller subproblems.

Let's consider an example with the input array [1, 2, 3, 4, 5]. We can define a function 'maxSumNonAdjacent' that takes the input array and returns the maximum sum of non-adjacent elements. We can use a dynamic programming approach by defining an 'dp' array that keeps track of the maximum sums we can obtain up to the i-th element of the input array.

To fill in the 'dp' array, we can use the following recurrence relation:

```
dp[i] = max(dp[i-1], dp[i-2] + arr[i])
```

where 'arr[i]' is the i-th element of the input array.

The idea behind this recurrence relation is that we can either include the i-th element in our non-adjacent subset, or we can exclude it. If we include the i-th element, then the maximum sum we can obtain is 'dp[i-2] + arr[i]', since we can't include adjacent elements. If we exclude the i-th element, then the maximum sum we can obtain is 'dp[i-1]'.

To compute the final maximum sum, we simply return 'dp[n-1]', where 'n' is the length of the input array.

Here's the Java code that implements this dynamic programming approach:

```java
public int maxSumNonAdjacent(int[] arr) {
    int n = arr.length;
    if (n == 0) {
        return 0;
    } else if (n == 1) {
        return arr[0];
    }

    int[] dp = new int[n];
    dp[0] = arr[0];
    dp[1] = Math.max(arr[0], arr[1]);

    for (int i = 2; i < n; i++) {
        dp[i] = Math.max(dp[i-1], dp[i-2] + arr[i]);
    }

    return dp[n-1];
}
```

For the input array [1, 2, 3, 4, 5], this code would return 9, which is the maximum sum we can obtain by selecting non-adjacent elements [1, 3, 5].

4.14   Solve the problem of finding the Shortest Common Superstring of a set of strings using dynamic programming.

The problem of finding the shortest common superstring of a set of strings is a classic problem in string manipulation and can be solved using dynamic programming. The basic idea is to use a table to store the lengths of the shortest common superstrings of all possible combinations of substrings from the set of input strings. We then can reconstruct the shortest common superstring by backtracking through the table.

Here's how to implement the solution using dynamic programming:

1. Build a graph whose vertices are the strings and the edges are the overlaps of the strings. An overlap occurs when the end of one string matches the beginning of another string.

2. Find the shortest path that visits every vertex exactly once. This is equivalent to finding the Hamiltonian path in the graph.

3. Once we have the shortest path, we can concatenate the strings in the order they appear on the path, skipping over the overlapping characters of adjacent strings.

4. If an overlapping character is found, we just keep the non-overlapping part.

5. Return the resulting superstring.

For example, let's say we are given the input strings "ACGT",

"CGTA", "GTAC", "TACG". We can build a graph with vertices "ACGT", "CGTA", "GTAC", "TACG" and edges between each pair of vertices that overlap.

```
ACGT   CGTA   GTAC   TACG
 |      |      |      |
CGTA   GTAC   ACGT   ACGT
 |      |      |      |
GTAC   TACG   CGTA   CGTA
 |      |      |      |
TACG   ACGT   TACG   GTAC
```

We can then use dynamic programming to solve this problem by creating a table of size $2^4 x4$ for all the possible combinations of the vertices and their lengths.

	ACGT	CGTA	GTAC	TACG
0000	0	0	0	0
0001	4	4	4	4
0010	4	4	4	4
0011	7	6	7	6
0100	4	4	4	4
0101	7	7	7	7
0110	7	7	7	7
0111	10	9	10	9
1000	4	4	4	4
1001	7	7	7	7
1010	7	7	7	7
1011	10	10	10	10
1100	7	7	7	7
1101	10	10	10	10
1110	10	10	10	10
1111	13	12	13	12

The cell at the bottom-right corner of the table shows the length of the shortest common superstring for all the input strings. We can then backtrack through the table to find the actual superstring by following the path with the shortest length. Using the same example, the optimal order of concatenating the strings together is "ACGTACGTA" which is the shortest common superstring for the given set of input strings.

Here's the Java code for the solution:

```java
public static String shortestCommonSuperstring(String[] strings) {
    int n = strings.length;
    int[][] dp = new int[1 << n][n];
    int[][] overlaps = new int[n][n];

    // Create overlaps graph
    for (int i = 0; i < n; i++) {
        for (int j = 0; j < n; j++) {
            if (i != j) {
                int p = 0;
                while (p < strings[i].length() && strings[j].
startsWith(strings[i].substring(p))) {
                    p++;
                }
                overlaps[i][j] = p;
            }
        }
    }

    // Populate dp table
    for (int i = 1; i < (1 << n); i++) {
        Arrays.fill(dp[i], Integer.MAX_VALUE);
        for (int j = 0; j < n; j++) {
            if ((i & (1 << j)) > 0) {
                if (i == 1 << j) {
                    dp[i][j] = strings[j].length();
                } else {
                    for (int k = 0; k < n; k++) {
                        if (k != j && (i & (1 << k)) > 0 && dp[i - (1
    << j)][k] != Integer.MAX_VALUE) {
                            dp[i][j] = Math.min(dp[i][j], dp[i - (1
    << j)][k] + strings[j].length() - overlaps[k][j]);
                        }
                    }
                }
            }
        }
    }

    // Trace back shortest path to reconstruct superstring
    int minIndex = 0, minVal = Integer.MAX_VALUE;
    for (int i = 0; i < n; i++) {
        if (dp[(1 << n) - 1][i] < minVal) {
            minIndex = i;
            minVal = dp[(1 << n) - 1][i];
        }
    }
    StringBuilder sb = new StringBuilder(strings[minIndex]);
    int used = 1 << minIndex;
    while (used < (1 << n)) {
        int next = -1;
        for (int i = 0; i < n; i++) {
            if ((used & (1 << i)) == 0 && dp[used][minIndex] == dp[
```

```
    used | (1 << i)][i] + strings[i].length() - overlaps[minIndex][i
    ]) {
                next = i;
                break;
            }
        }
        sb.append(strings[next].substring(overlaps[minIndex][next]));
        used |= 1 << next;
        minIndex = next;
    }
    return sb.toString();
}
```

4.15 Implement the solution to the Cutting a Rod with Maximum Product problem using dynamic programming.

The Cutting a Rod with Maximum Product problem is to find the maximum product we can get by cutting a rod of length n into smaller pieces of integral length and selling them. Each length has a corresponding price value. We want to find the best way to cut the rod so that we get the maximum product by multiplying the prices of the pieces.

Here's the dynamic programming solution to the problem:

1. Define the state: Let dp[i] be the maximum product we can get by cutting a rod of length i.

2. Define the base case: dp[0] = 1 (if the length of the rod is 0, the maximum product we can get is 1, since we can sell nothing and get nothing.)

3. Define the transition function: For each rod length i, we need to consider all possible cuts from 1 to i-1. For each cut j,

we can split the rod into two pieces - one of length j and the other of length i-j. The maximum product we can get from this split is the product of the maximum product we can get from the pieces of length j and i-j, respectively. We want to find the best cut j that gives us the maximum product, and assign that value to dp[i]. In other words:

```
dp[i] = max(dp[i], max(j * (i-j), dp[j] * dp[i-j]))
```

4. Return dp[n] as the answer: dp[n] will contain the maximum product we can get by cutting a rod of length n into smaller pieces.

Here's the Java code for the solution:

```java
public int maxProduct(int[] prices, int n) {
    int[] dp = new int[n+1];
    dp[0] = 1;

    for (int i = 1; i <= n; i++) {
        for (int j = 1; j < i; j++) { // check all possible cuts
            dp[i] = Math.max(dp[i], Math.max(j * (i-j), dp[j] * dp[i-
j]));
        }

        // check if selling the rod as a single piece is more
profitable
        dp[i] = Math.max(dp[i], prices[i-1]);
    }

    return dp[n];
}
```

In this code, 'prices' is an array containing the prices of different lengths of the rod, and 'n' is the length of the rod we want to cut. We initialize 'dp[0]' to 1, since if the length of the rod is 0, we can't sell anything and still get some product.

We then loop over all possible rod lengths from 1 to 'n'. For each rod length 'i', we loop over all possible cuts 'j' from 1 to 'i-1'. For each cut, we calculate the maximum product we can get by multiplying the maximum products of the pieces of length 'j' and 'i-j', and taking the maximum of that value and the current value of 'dp[i]'.

Finally, we also check if selling the rod as a single piece (i.e., not cutting it at all) yields a higher profit than any of the cuts. We take the maximum of all these values and return it as the result.

4.16 How can you use dynamic programming to solve the Count Derangements problem? Implement the solution.

The Count Derangements problem can be stated as follows: given a set of n elements, how many permutations of the set exist where no element appears in its original position? A permutation that satisfies this condition is called a derangement.

Dynamic programming can be used to solve this problem because the solution to the problem depends on the solution to its smaller subproblems. Specifically, we can use memoization to store the results of subproblems and use them to avoid redundant computations.

Let d(n) be the number of derangements of a set of n elements. We can express the number of derangements for n in terms of its solutions for smaller problems. For example, we can consider what happens when we place the first element in any of the n - 1 remaining positions. If we place it in position i, then we have two options for placing the element that was initially in position i: either place it in the first position, which means that we have a subproblem with n - 2 elements, or we place it somewhere other than the first position, which means that we have a subproblem with n - 1 elements. In this analysis, we can see that the solution to the problem for n depends on the solutions to two smaller subproblems (n - 1 and n - 2).

Using memoization, we can avoid computing the same subproblems multiple times. We can create an array or hashmap where we store the solutions to subproblems as we compute them, so that we can reuse them later if necessary. We can start with the base cases $d(0) = 1$ and $d(1) = 0$, and compute the solutions for larger values of n recursively as follows:

```
public static int countDerangementsMemoized(int n, Map<Integer,
    Integer> memo) {
    if (n == 0) {
        return 1;
    } else if (n == 1) {
        return 0;
    } else if (memo.containsKey(n)) {
        return memo.get(n);
    } else {
        int derangements = (n - 1) * (countDerangementsMemoized(n -
    1, memo) + countDerangementsMemoized(n - 2, memo));
        memo.put(n, derangements);
        return derangements;
    }
}
```

Here, we use a Map<Integer, Integer> to store the results of previously computed subproblems. If the solution for the subproblem n is already in the memo, we simply return it; otherwise, we compute it recursively using the formula for computing the derangements.

To call this function, we can use:

```
int n = 5;
Map<Integer, Integer> memo = new HashMap<>();
int derangements = countDerangementsMemoized(n, memo);
```

```
System.out.println("Number␣of␣derangements␣of␣" + n + "␣elements:␣" +
    derangements);
```

This implementation has a time complexity of $O(n)$, as each subproblem is computed only once and stored in the memo. Without memoization, the time complexity would be $O(2^n)$, as we would need to compute each subproblem multiple times.

4.17   Solve the Count Number of Ways to Cover a Distance problem using dynamic programming.

The problem of counting the number of ways to cover a distance can be stated as follows: Given a distance 'dist', count total number of ways to cover the distance with 1, 2, or 3 steps at a time.

For example, if 'dist = 3', the possible ways to cover the distance are:

- {1, 1, 1}
- {1, 2}
- {2, 1}
- {3}

The brute force solution for this problem is to use recursion and try all possible combinations of steps. However, this solution has a high time complexity because it generates many overlapping subproblems. Therefore, dynamic programming is a good approach to solve this problem.

We will use a one-dimensional integer array 'ways' of size 'dist+1'. The 'i'-th element of the array is the number of ways to cover 'i' distance. The base cases are:

```
- `ways[0] = 1` (there is only one way to cover 0 distance)
- `ways[1] = 1` (there is only one way to cover 1 distance)
- `ways[2] = 2` (there are two ways to cover 2 distance: {1, 1} and
    {2})
```

The recursive formula for calculating 'ways[i]' is:

```
ways[i] = ways[i-1] + ways[i-2] + ways[i-3]
```

The reason for this formula is that we can reach distance 'i' by taking a step of size 1, 2, or 3 from distance 'i-1', 'i-2', or 'i-3', respectively. Therefore, the total number of ways to reach 'i' is the sum of the total number of ways to reach 'i-1', 'i-2', and 'i-3'.

Here's the Java code that implements this solution:

```java
public int countWays(int dist) {
    int[] ways = new int[dist+1];
    ways[0] = 1;
    ways[1] = 1;
    ways[2] = 2;
    for (int i = 3; i <= dist; i++) {
        ways[i] = ways[i-1] + ways[i-2] + ways[i-3];
    }
    return ways[dist];
}
```

For example, if we call 'countWays(3)', the function returns 4 because there are 4 ways to cover a distance of 3.

4.18   Implement the solution to the Longest Path in a Directed Acyclic Graph (DAG) problem using dynamic programming.

The Longest Path in a Directed Acyclic Graph problem asks us to find the longest simple path in a directed acyclic graph. A simple path is a path with no repeated vertices.

One approach to solve this problem is to use dynamic programming. We can define an array 'dp' where 'dp[i]' represents the length of the longest path starting from vertex 'i'. We can then iterate over every vertex in the graph and compute 'dp[i]' using the following recurrence relation:

```
dp[i] = max(dp[j] + 1) for every edge (i, j) in the graph
```

Here, we add 1 to the longest path starting from vertex 'j' and going through edge '(i, j)' to get the longest path starting from vertex 'i'.

Once we have computed 'dp[i]' for every vertex 'i', the answer will be the maximum value in the 'dp' array.

Here is the Java code to implement this solution:

```java
import java.util.*;

public class LongestPathDAG {
    static List<Integer>[] adj;
    static int n;

    public static void main(String[] args) {
        Scanner sc = new Scanner(System.in);
        n = sc.nextInt(); // number of vertices
        int m = sc.nextInt(); // number of edges
        adj = new ArrayList[n];
        for (int i = 0; i < n; i++) {
```

```
            adj[i] = new ArrayList<>();
        }
        for (int i = 0; i < m; i++) {
            int a = sc.nextInt();
            int b = sc.nextInt();
            adj[a].add(b);
        }
        int ans = longestPath();
        System.out.println(ans);
    }

    static int longestPath() {
        int[] dp = new int[n];
        Arrays.fill(dp, -1);
        for (int i = 0; i < n; i++) {
            if (dp[i] == -1) {
                dfs(i, dp);
            }
        }
        int ans = 0;
        for (int i = 0; i < n; i++) {
            ans = Math.max(ans, dp[i]);
        }
        return ans;
    }

    static void dfs(int u, int[] dp) {
        dp[u] = 0;
        for (int v : adj[u]) {
            if (dp[v] == -1) {
                dfs(v, dp);
            }
            dp[u] = Math.max(dp[u], dp[v] + 1);
        }
    }
}
```

The 'longestPath' function computes the 'dp' array using the recurrence relation described above. It also calls the 'dfs' function to do a depth-first search of the graph and ensure that every vertex is visited.

The 'dfs' function updates the 'dp' array for vertex 'u' by iterating over all its neighbors 'v'. If we haven't computed the longest path starting from 'v', we first call 'dfs(v, dp)'. We then update 'dp[u]' by taking the maximum of its current value and the longest path starting from 'v' plus 1.

The main function reads in the input graph (in the form of a list of directed edges) and calls 'longestPath' to compute the answer. It then prints the answer to the console.

4.19 Discuss the concept of state compression in dynamic programming with an example.

State compression is a technique used in dynamic programming algorithms to reduce the memory requirements by compressing the state information required to calculate the optimal solution. In general, dynamic programming algorithms work by storing the intermediate results of sub-problems in memory and then using these results to calculate the optimal solution for a larger problem. However, if the state information required to describe the sub-problems is too large, this can quickly become impractical.

To understand the concept of state compression, consider the example of the Knapsack problem. In this problem, we are given a set of items, each with a weight and a value, and a knapsack with a maximum weight capacity. The task is to find the subset of items that can be packed into the knapsack with the highest total value.

A straightforward dynamic programming solution to this problem would involve creating a two-dimensional table where the rows represent the items, and the columns represent the weight capacities of the knapsack. We would then iterate through each

item, and for each item, we would iterate through each weight
capacity, filling in the table based on whether or not we include
the item in the knapsack:

```
for (int i = 0; i < items.length; i++) {
  for (int j = 0; j <= maxCapacity; j++) {
    if (items[i].weight > j) {
      // the item cannot be included, so use the value from the
      previous item
      table[i][j] = table[i-1][j];
    } else {
      // choose whether to include the item or not
      int valueWithItem = items[i].value + table[i-1][j-items[i].
      weight];
      int valueWithoutItem = table[i-1][j];
      table[i][j] = Math.max(valueWithItem, valueWithoutItem);
    }
  }
}
```

In this implementation, the state information needed to describe a sub-problem is the item index and the weight capacity.
However, if the number of items or the maximum capacity is
very large, this two-dimensional table could be too large to fit
in memory.

One way to reduce the memory requirements of this algorithm
is to use state compression. Instead of storing the entire table,
we can store only the last row of the table and overwrite it as
we move through the items. This is possible because each row
depends only on the row above it. We can also reorder the
items in descending order of weight, so we can break out of the
inner loop as soon as we reach a point where the remaining
capacity is less than the weight of the next item. Here's the
revised implementation:

```
Arrays.sort(items, (a, b) -> Integer.compare(b.weight, a.weight));
int[] table = new int[maxCapacity + 1];
for (int i = 0; i < items.length; i++) {
  for (int j = maxCapacity; j >= items[i].weight; j--) {
    int valueWithItem = items[i].value + table[j-items[i].weight];
```

```
    int valueWithoutItem = table[j];
    table[j] = Math.max(valueWithItem, valueWithoutItem);
  }
}
```

In this implementation, we have compressed the state information required to describe a sub-problem into a one-dimensional array containing the maximum value of each weight capacity. By using state compression and reordering the items, we can reduce the memory requirements of this algorithm from $O(NW)$ to $O(W)$, where N is the number of items and W is the maximum weight capacity.

Overall, state compression is an essential technique to consider when dealing with large dynamic programming problems, as it allows us to reduce the memory requirements and optimize our algorithms for space complexity.

4.20 Solve the problem of finding the Maximum Size Square Sub-Matrix with all 1s in a binary matrix using dynamic programming.

The problem of finding the Maximum Size Square Sub-Matrix with all 1s in a binary matrix using dynamic programming can be solved using a bottom-up approach.

Let 'maxSize' be the variable that holds the size of the largest square sub-matrix of all 1s that is found so far.

We can define a 2D array 'dp[][]' such that 'dp[i][j]' represents the size of the largest square sub-matrix with all 1s that has its bottom-right corner at 'matrix[i][j]'.

We can initialize the first row and first column of 'dp[][]' with the corresponding values of 'matrix[][]', since any square sub-matrix at the edges of the matrix can only have a size of 1.

Then, for each cell 'dp[i][j]', if 'matrix[i][j]' is 1, we can set 'dp[i][j]' to 'min(dp[i-1][j], dp[i][j-1], dp[i-1][j-1]) + 1'. This is because the size of the largest square sub-matrix with all 1s that has its bottom-right corner at 'matrix[i][j]' is determined by the minimum of its top, left, and diagonal neighbors.

As we fill in the 'dp[][]' array, we can also update 'maxSize' accordingly.

Here's a Java implementation of the algorithm:

```java
public int findMaxSquareSubmatrix(int[][] matrix) {
    int n = matrix.length;
    int m = matrix[0].length;
    int maxSize = 0;
    int[][] dp = new int[n][m];

    // Initialize first row and first column of dp array
    for (int i = 0; i < n; i++) {
        dp[i][0] = matrix[i][0];
        maxSize = Math.max(maxSize, dp[i][0]);
    }
    for (int j = 0; j < m; j++) {
        dp[0][j] = matrix[0][j];
        maxSize = Math.max(maxSize, dp[0][j]);
    }

    // Fill in the rest of the dp array and update maxSize
    for (int i = 1; i < n; i++) {
        for (int j = 1; j < m; j++) {
            if (matrix[i][j] == 1) {
                dp[i][j] = Math.min(dp[i-1][j], Math.min(dp[i][j-1],
    dp[i-1][j-1])) + 1;
                maxSize = Math.max(maxSize, dp[i][j]);
            }
        }
    }

    return maxSize * maxSize; // return area of largest square sub-
```

```
    matrix
}
```

Let's consider an example to understand the algorithm better. Suppose we have the following binary matrix:

```
1 0 0 1 1 1
1 1 1 1 1 1
0 1 1 1 0 0
0 1 1 1 1 0
1 1 1 1 1 1
0 0 1 1 1 0
```

We can apply the above algorithm to find the maximum size square sub-matrix with all 1s as follows:

1. Initialize 'dp[][]' and 'maxSize':

```
dp[][] = 1 0 0 1 1 1
         1 1 1 1 1 1
         0 0 0 0 0 0
         0 0 0 0 0 0
         1 0 0 0 0 0
         0 0 0 0 0 0

maxSize = 1
```

2. Fill in first row and first column of 'dp[][]':

```
dp[][] = 1 0 0 1 1 1
         1 1 1 1 1 1
         0 0 0 0 0 0
         0 0 0 0 0 0
         1 0 0 0 0 0
         0 0 0 0 0 0

maxSize = 1
```

3. Fill in the rest of 'dp[][]' and update 'maxSize':

```
dp[][] = 1 0 0 1 1 1
         1 1 1 1 1 1
         0 1 1 1 0 0
         0 1 2 2 1 0
         1 2 2 3 2 1
         0 0 1 2 2 0

maxSize = 3
```

4. Return 'maxSize * maxSize' as the area of the largest square sub-matrix:

```
maxSize = 3
Area of largest square sub-matrix = maxSize * maxSize = 9
```

Therefore, the maximum size square sub-matrix with all 1s in the binary matrix is of size 3 x 3 and its area is 9.

Chapter 5

Expert

5.1 Implement the solution to the Optimal File Merge Patterns problem using dynamic programming.

The Optimal File Merge Patterns problem involves finding the minimum cost to merge multiple files of different sizes into a single file. Given n files of sizes s1, s2, ..., sn, the cost to merge any two files i and j is si + sj. The problem is to find the minimum cost to merge all the files.

Dynamic programming can be used to solve this problem efficiently. We can define a table M where M[i][j] represents the minimum cost to merge files from i to j. The base case is when i=j, in which case the minimum cost is 0. For all other cases, the minimum cost can be computed recursively:

```
M[i][j] = min(M[i][k] + M[k+1][j] + sum(s[i..j])) for i <= k < j
```

Here, 'sum(s[i..j])' represents the sum of sizes of all files from i
to j.

In the above recursive formula, we try all possible ways to
divide the files from i to j into two groups (i to k and k+1 to
j), and compute the cost of merging each group separately and
then merging the two resulting groups. We take the minimum
of all such costs as the optimal cost.

The time complexity of this algorithm is $O(n^3)$ and the space
complexity is also $O(n^2)$.

Here's the Java code for implementing this algorithm using
dynamic programming:

```java
public static int optimalMerge(int[] sizes) {
    int n = sizes.length;
    int[][] M = new int[n][n];

    // base case
    for (int i = 0; i < n; i++) {
        M[i][i] = 0;
    }

    // fill the table diagonally
    for (int len = 2; len <= n; len++) {
        for (int i = 0; i <= n - len; i++) {
            int j = i + len - 1;
            int minCost = Integer.MAX_VALUE;

            // try all possible ways to divide the files into two
        groups
            for (int k = i; k < j; k++) {
                int cost = M[i][k] + M[k+1][j] + sum(sizes, i, j);
                minCost = Math.min(minCost, cost);
            }

            M[i][j] = minCost;
        }
    }

    return M[0][n-1];
}

private static int sum(int[] sizes, int i, int j) {
    int sum = 0;
    for (int k = i; k <= j; k++) {
```

```
        sum += sizes[k];
    }
    return sum;
}
```

Here's an example of how to use this function:

```
int[] sizes = {2, 3, 4, 5, 6};
int cost = optimalMerge(sizes);
System.out.println(cost); // expected output: 58
```

In this example, we have 5 files of sizes 2, 3, 4, 5, and 6. The minimum cost to merge them is 58, which can be achieved by merging files 1 and 2, then files 3 and 4, and finally merging the resulting two groups of files.

5.2   Solve the problem of finding the Minimum Cost Polygon Triangulation using dynamic programming.

The Minimum Cost Polygon Triangulation problem involves dividing a given polygon into a minimum number of triangles, such that the total cost of triangulation is minimized. The cost of triangulation is defined as the sum of the lengths of the diagonals of all triangles in the triangulation.

To solve this problem using dynamic programming, we can use a table to store the minimum cost of triangulation for all possible subproblems. Let's define M(i,j) as the minimum cost of triangulating the polygon formed by vertices i+1, i+2, ..., j-1, j in order.

To calculate M(i,j), we can consider all possible diagonals from vertex i+1 to j-1, and calculate the cost of triangulation by adding the cost of the current diagonal to the cost of triangulating the two resulting sub-polygons on either side of the diagonal. We can choose the diagonal with the minimum cost, and store it in our table as the minimum cost for the subproblem M(i,j).

The base case for the recursion is when i and j are adjacent vertices, in which case there are no diagonals to consider and the cost is 0.

The final answer for the minimum cost of triangulation can be found in M(0,n), where n is the total number of vertices in the polygon.

Here's the Java code for this approach:

```java
public static double minimumCostPolygonTriangulation(double[] x,
    double[] y) {
    int n = x.length;
    double[][] dp = new double[n][n];
    for (int gap = 3; gap < n; gap++) {
        for (int i = 0; i < n - gap; i++) {
            int j = i + gap;
            dp[i][j] = Double.MAX_VALUE;
            for (int k = i + 1; k < j; k++) {
                dp[i][j] = Math.min(dp[i][j], dp[i][k] + dp[k][j] +
cost(x[i], y[i], x[j], y[j], x[k], y[k]));
            }
        }
    }
    return dp[0][n - 1];
}

public static double cost(double x1, double y1, double x2, double y2,
    double x3, double y3) {
    return Math.sqrt((x1 - x2) * (x1 - x2) + (y1 - y2) * (y1 - y2)) +
        Math.sqrt((x1 - x3) * (x1 - x3) + (y1 - y3) * (y1 - y3)) +
        Math.sqrt((x2 - x3) * (x2 - x3) + (y2 - y3) * (y2 - y3));
}
```

In this code, we iterate over all possible subproblems of increasing size gap, and for each subproblem formed by vertices i+1 to j-1, we calculate the minimum cost by considering all possible diagonals from vertex i+1 to j-1. The cost function calculates the length of the diagonal and adds it to the cost of triangulating the two sub-polygons resulting from the diagonal. The final answer is stored in the table cell dp[0][n-1]. The time complexity of this algorithm is $O(n^3)$, since we need to consider all possible subproblems for all possible diagonals.

5.3   Discuss the limitations of dynamic programming and provide an example where it might not be the most efficient approach.

While dynamic programming is a powerful technique for solving many optimization problems, it has some limitations that can make it less efficient or difficult to apply in certain cases. Some of the limitations are:

1. Overhead Costs: Dynamic programming typically has significant overhead costs, especially when there are a large number of subproblems to solve. This can make it less efficient than other techniques in some cases.

2. Memory Consumption: Dynamic programming algorithms often require a lot of memory to store intermediate results, which can make them impractical or impossible to use in some situations.

3. Difficulty of Implementation: Dynamic programming algorithms can be complex and difficult to implement correctly,

especially when dealing with complex problems or variations that may arise in real-world applications.

One example where dynamic programming may not be the most efficient approach is in certain types of graph problems. For instance, consider the problem of computing the shortest path between two nodes in a graph with negative edges. While dynamic programming can be used to solve this problem, it cannot handle negative cycles in the graph as it assumes that the optimal solution is obtained by combining optimal solutions to subproblems. In such a case, using the Bellman-Ford algorithm, which detects negative cycles in addition to finding the shortest path, might be a more efficient approach.

Another example where dynamic programming may not be the most efficient approach is in problems where the optimal solution involves selecting a subset of the input rather than organizing it in a sequential manner. One such example is the Knapsack problem, where the objective is to maximize the value of items placed into a knapsack of given capacity. In this case, using dynamic programming may result in a lengthy execution time and a large memory footprint. Instead, the Greedy algorithm can be used to solve the same problem in a more efficient manner.

5.4   Implement the solution to the Text Justification problem using dynamic programming.

The Text Justification problem is a classic example of a dynamic programming problem. Given a sequence of words and a line width, we want to minimize the "badness" of the text justification. The badness is defined as the sum of the cubes of the number of spaces needed to pad out a line, so we want to minimize the sum of the cubes of the number of spaces needed to justify all the lines.

The dynamic programming solution to Text Justification can be solved in two steps:

Step 1: Compute the cost of every possible line break.

The first step is to compute the cost of every possible line break. This can be done using a dynamic programming table where the cost of a line from i to j is stored in the table. We start with the last word in the sequence and work our way backwards, computing the cost of each possible line break from i to j. The cost of a line is defined as $(line\_width - total\_words\_width)^3$, where total_words_width is the sum of the widths of the words in the line.

We can compute the cost of every possible line break using a nested loop:

```
int[][] cost = new int[n][n];
for (int i = n-1; i >= 0; i--) {
    for (int j = i; j < n; j++) {
        int total_width = get_total_width(i, j);
        if (total_width > line_width) {
            cost[i][j] = Integer.MAX_VALUE;
        } else if (j == n-1) {
            cost[i][j] = (int) Math.pow(line_width - total_width, 3);
        } else {
            for (int k = j+1; k < n; k++) {
                int new_cost = cost[j+1][k] + (int) Math.pow(
    line_width - total_width, 3);
                if (new_cost < cost[i][j]) {
                    cost[i][j] = new_cost;
                }
            }
        }
    }
}
```

```
}
```

In this code, we start with the last word in the sequence (i.e.,
j = n-1) and work our way backwards. If the total width of
the words from i to j exceeds the line width, we set the cost
to infinity since this line cannot be justified. Otherwise, we
compute the cost of the line as described above. If j is the
last word in the sequence, there is only one line so the cost is
simply the badness of that line. If j is not the last word in the
sequence, we try every possible line break after j and choose
the one with the minimum cost.

Step 2: Compute the optimal solution.

The second step is to compute the optimal solution using the
table of costs that we computed in Step 1. We start at the beginning of the sequence and work our way through, computing
the optimal line breaks using the previously computed costs.

```
int[] linebreaks = new int[n];
int[] optimal_costs = new int[n];
for (int i = n-1; i >= 0; i--) {
    int min_cost = Integer.MAX_VALUE;
    int min_k = n-1;
    for (int j = i; j < n; j++) {
        int cost = cost[i][j];
        if (cost != Integer.MAX_VALUE) {
            int total_cost = cost + (j == n-1 ? 0 : optimal_costs[j
    +1]);
            if (total_cost < min_cost) {
                min_cost = total_cost;
                min_k = j;
            }
        }
    }
    optimal_costs[i] = min_cost;
    linebreaks[i] = min_k;
}
```

In this code, we start at the beginning of the sequence and work
our way through, computing the optimal line breaks using the

previously computed costs. For each i, we try every possible line break to find the one with the minimum cost. If there is no valid line break from i (i.e., the cost is infinity), we set the optimal cost to infinity as well. Otherwise, we compute the total cost (i.e., the current line's cost plus the optimal cost from the next line) and check if it is smaller than the current minimum cost. If it is, we update the minimum cost and the corresponding line break index.

After the final iteration, the array of line breaks contains the optimal line breaks for the text justification.

Here is the complete code:

```
public static List<String> justify(String[] words, int line_width) {
    int n = words.length;

    // Step 1: Compute the cost of every possible line break.
    int[][] cost = new int[n][n];
    for (int i = n-1; i >= 0; i--) {
        for (int j = i; j < n; j++) {
            int total_width = get_total_width(words, i, j);
            if (total_width > line_width) {
                cost[i][j] = Integer.MAX_VALUE;
            } else if (j == n-1) {
                cost[i][j] = (int) Math.pow(line_width - total_width,
    3);
            } else {
                for (int k = j+1; k < n; k++) {
                    int new_cost = cost[j+1][k] + (int) Math.pow(
    line_width - total_width, 3);
                    if (new_cost < cost[i][j]) {
                        cost[i][j] = new_cost;
                    }
                }
            }
        }
    }

    // Step 2: Compute the optimal solution.
    int[] linebreaks = new int[n];
    int[] optimal_costs = new int[n];
    for (int i = n-1; i >= 0; i--) {
        int min_cost = Integer.MAX_VALUE;
        int min_k = n-1;
        for (int j = i; j < n; j++) {
```

```
            int cost_ij = cost[i][j];
            if (cost_ij != Integer.MAX_VALUE) {
                int total_cost = cost_ij + (j == n-1 ? 0 :
      optimal_costs[j+1]);
                if (total_cost < min_cost) {
                    min_cost = total_cost;
                    min_k = j;
                }
            }
        }
        optimal_costs[i] = min_cost;
        linebreaks[i] = min_k;
    }

    // Construct the lines.
    List<String> lines = new ArrayList<>();
    int i = 0;
    while (i < n) {
        int j = linebreaks[i];
        int width = get_total_width(words, i, j);
        StringBuilder line = new StringBuilder();
        line.append(words[i]);
        for (int k = i+1; k <= j; k++) {
            line.append('␣');
            line.append(words[k]);
        }
        for (int k = 0; k < line_width - width; k++) {
            line.append('␣');
        }
        lines.add(line.toString());
        i = j+1;
    }
    return lines;
}

private static int get_total_width(String[] words, int i, int j) {
    int width = j - i;  // Space width.
    for (int k = i; k <= j; k++) {
        width += words[k].length();
    }
    return width;
}
```

To use the above code, simply call 'justify(words, line_width)'
where 'words' is an array of strings representing the words in
the text and 'line_width' is the desired line width. The function returns a list of strings representing the lines of justified
text.

5.5   How can dynamic programming be applied to solve the K-Palindrome problem? Implement the solution.

The K-Palindrome problem is a variant of the classic palindrome problem, where instead of finding whether a string is a palindrome or not, we need to find if a string can be converted into a palindrome by changing at most k characters.

Dynamic programming is an excellent approach to solve problems like this because it allows us to break down the larger problem into smaller subproblems and reuse the precomputed results multiple times.

Here's an approach to solve the K-Palindrome problem using dynamic programming:

1. We first define a two-dimensional array 'dp[][]', where 'dp[i][j]' represents whether the substring from index 'i' to index 'j' of the given string is a palindrome or not.

2. We then initialize the diagonal elements of the array to 1, as every substring of length 1 is a palindrome.

3. Next, we iterate through the array to fill in the remaining elements, starting with the substrings of length 2 and increasing the length for each iteration.

4. While iterating, we compare the characters at the start and end of the substring. If they are the same, we check whether the substring 'dp[i+1][j-1]' is a palindrome or not, and set 'dp[i][j]' accordingly.

5. If the characters at the start and end of the substring are different, we take the minimum of 'dp[i+1][j]' and 'dp[i][j-1]' and add 1. This is because, since we can only modify at most k characters to make it a palindrome, we need to keep track of the number of modifications we make as we go along.

6. Finally, if 'dp[0][n-1] <= 2*k', where 'n' is the length of the input string, we can say that the string can be converted into a palindrome by changing at most k characters.

Here's the Java code that implements this algorithm:

```java
public static boolean isKPalindrome(String s, int k) {
    int n = s.length();
    int[][] dp = new int[n][n];

    for (int i = 0; i < n; i++) {
        dp[i][i] = 1;
    }

    for (int len = 2; len <= n; len++) {
        for (int i = 0; i <= n - len; i++) {
            int j = i + len - 1;
            if (s.charAt(i) == s.charAt(j)) {
                if (len == 2) {
                    dp[i][j] = 2;
                } else {
                    dp[i][j] = dp[i+1][j-1] + 2;
                }
            } else {
                dp[i][j] = Math.max(dp[i+1][j], dp[i][j-1]);
            }
        }
    }

    return n - dp[0][n-1] <= k * 2;
}
```

Let's test this function with an example:

```java
String s = "abcdba";
int k = 1;
System.out.println(isKPalindrome(s, k));   // Output: true
```

In this example, the input string 'abcdba' can be converted

into a palindrome by changing just one character. We get the expected output of 'true' from our function.

5.6   Solve the Maximum Profit with K Transactions problem using dynamic programming.

The Maximum Profit with K Transactions is a classic dynamic programming problem that asks us to find the maximum profit that can be obtained by purchasing and selling stocks up to k times, with restrictions that we cannot sell before we buy and cannot have more than one transaction ongoing at any point in time.

To solve this problem using dynamic programming, we can use a 2D array to keep track of the maximum profit that can be obtained up to each transaction and each day. Let's call this array "dp."

The first dimension of "dp" represents the number of transactions made so far, and the second dimension represents the current day. For example, "dp[i][j]" will represent the maximum profit that can be obtained up to and including the jth day, using exactly i transactions.

To compute the value of "dp[i][j]," we consider two cases:

1. We don't make a transaction on the jth day. In this case, the value of "dp[i][j]" is the same as "dp[i][j-1]" since we don't change anything by not making any trades.

2. We make a transaction on the jth day. In this case, we

need to determine the maximum profit that can be obtained by purchasing a stock on any day "m" $<=$ "j" and selling it on day "j." We can compute the profit by subtracting the stock's purchase price from its selling price.

To do this, we can iterate over all possible days "m" less than or equal to "j." For each "m," we can compute the maximum profit that can be obtained up to day "m-1" using "i-1" transactions (since we're using one more transaction than in our current state), and then add the profit gained from purchasing the stock on day "m" and selling it on day "j."

By taking the maximum over all possible values of "m," we obtain the maximum profit that can be obtained with i transactions and selling on the jth day, allowing us to update "dp[i][j]."

Finally, to solve the problem, we return the value of "dp[k][n-1]," where "n" is the length of the given prices array.

Here's the Java code, assume prices is a given array of prices of stocks on each day:

```java
public int maxProfit(int k, int[] prices) {
    if (prices == null || prices.length == 0) {
        return 0;
    }

    int n = prices.length;
    int[][] dp = new int[k+1][n];

    for (int i = 1; i <= k; i++) {
        int maxProfit = -prices[0];
        for (int j = 1; j < n; j++) {
            dp[i][j] = Math.max(dp[i][j-1], prices[j] + maxProfit);
            maxProfit = Math.max(maxProfit, dp[i-1][j-1] - prices[j])
    ;
        }
    }

    return dp[k][n-1];
}
```

In this code, we initialize the first row of "dp" to be 0, since we cannot make any transactions with 0 days. Then, we iterate over each pair (i, j), starting from (1, 1) to compute "dp[i][j]" using the two cases described above. Once the iteration is complete, "dp[k][n-1]" will contain the maximum profit that can be obtained up to the nth day with k transactions.

5.7 Implement the solution to the Maximum Sum Subarray with Non-Overlapping Elements problem using dynamic programming.

The Maximum Sum Subarray with Non-Overlapping Elements problem states that given an array of integers and a value k, we need to find the maximum sum of k non-overlapping subarrays in the array.

We can solve this problem using dynamic programming by computing the maximum sum subarray with non-overlapping elements considering the first i elements of the array for each value of i. For each i, we will compute the maximum sum of k non-overlapping subarrays ending at i.

Let's define an array dp where dp[i][j] represents the maximum sum of j non-overlapping subarrays ending at i. For each i, we can compute dp[i][j] using the recurrence relation:

```
dp[i][j] = max(dp[i-1][j], dp[i-k][j-1] + sum(arr[i-k+1:i+1]))
```

Here, dp[i-1][j] represents the maximum sum of j non-overlapping subarrays ending at i-1. If we choose not to include the current element (i.e., arr[i]), then the maximum sum of j non-overlapping subarrays ending at i will be equal to dp[i-1][j].

On the other hand, dp[i-k][j-1] + sum(arr[i-k+1:i+1]) represents the maximum sum of j-1 non-overlapping subarrays ending at i-k, plus the sum of the k elements from i-k+1 to i. If we choose to include the current element, then we can only consider the subarrays that end at i-k, since we need non-overlapping subarrays. Therefore, the maximum sum of j non-overlapping subarrays ending at i will be equal to dp[i-k][j-1] + sum(arr[i-k+1:i+1]).

Finally, the answer to the problem will be the maximum value in dp[n-1][k], where n is the length of the array.

Here's the Java code that implements the above dynamic programming solution to the Maximum Sum Subarray with Non-Overlapping Elements:

```java
public int maxSumSubarray(int[] arr, int k) {
    int n = arr.length;
    int[][] dp = new int[n][k+1];

    for (int j = 1; j <= k; j++) {
        for (int i = j-1; i < n; i++) {
            if (j == 1) {
                dp[i][j] = Math.max(arr[i], (i > 0 ? dp[i-1][j] : 0))
    ;
            } else {
                dp[i][j] = (i > j-2 ? dp[i-j+1][j-1] : 0) + arr[i];
                dp[i][j] = Math.max(dp[i][j], dp[i-1][j]);
            }
        }
    }

    return dp[n-1][k];
}
```

The time complexity of the above solution is O(nk), where n is the length of the input array and k is the number of non-overlapping subarrays we need to find.

5.8 Discuss the concept of rolling hash and how it can be used to optimize dynamic programming solutions.

Rolling hash is a technique that is frequently used in dynamic programming to optimize the time complexities of algorithms that require string or array manipulation. It can be defined as a hash function that allows for the incremental calculation of a hash value for a string as more characters are added or removed from it.

In a typical dynamic programming solution, we often use a table to store the intermediate results of subproblems. However, precomputing hash values for these subproblems at the beginning of the algorithm can be computationally expensive. Rolling hash offers an alternative to calculating hash values for each subproblem by manipulating previously calculated hash values.

The basic idea behind a rolling hash is to treat a string or an array as a sequence of integers and use a formula to compute the hash value of each contiguous subarray. A common formula for implementing rolling hash is the polynomial hash function.

For example, for a string S of length n, with characters S[0], S[1], , S[n-1], a polynomial hash function can be defined as follows:

```
hash(S) = (S[0]*p^(n-1) + S[1]*p^(n-2) +  + S[n-1]*p^0) mod m
```

where p is a prime number and m is a large constant.

The key feature of the polynomial hash function is that it allows for the efficient computation of hash values for a subarray of S[i..j] based on the hash value of the prefix S[0..i-1]. This can be achieved using the following formula:

```
hash(S[i..j]) = (hash(S[0..j]) - hash(S[0..i-1]) * p^(j-i+1)) mod m
```

By using this formula, we can compute the hash value for each subarray of S in O(n) time, which is much more efficient than computing the hash value for each subarray from scratch.

Rolling hash can be especially useful in dynamic programming problems that involve comparing substrings or subarrays. For example, a common problem in bioinformatics is the longest common substring problem. Given two strings s and t, the task is to find the longest common substring of s and t.

A brute force solution to this problem would require $O(n^3)$ time, where n is the length of the longer string. However, the use of a rolling hash can reduce the time complexity to $O(n^2 log n)$, making it much more efficient.

Other examples of dynamic programming problems that can be optimized with the use of a rolling hash include the longest palindromic substring problem and the string edit distance problem.

In Java, a simple implementation of rolling hash for strings may look like this:

```java
public long rollingHash(String s) {
    int p = 31;
    int m = 1_000_000_007;
    long hash = 0;
    long powP = 1;
    for (char c : s.toCharArray()) {
        hash = (hash + (c - 'a' + 1) * powP) % m;
        powP = (powP * p) % m;
    }
    return hash;
```

}

This implementation returns the hash value of a string s using the polynomial hash function with p = 31 and m = 1,000,000,007. The hash value is calculated incrementally by adding the contribution of each character to the hash value using the formula 'hash = (hash + (c - 'a' + 1) * powP) % m', where c is the character, 'a' is subtracted to convert the character to a 1-based indexing, and powP is a precomputed value of p^i.

5.9   Solve the Balanced Partition problem using dynamic programming.

The Balanced Partition problem can be briefly defined as follows: Given a set of integers, divide it into two subsets such that the difference between the sum of the elements in each subset is minimized.

This problem can be solved using dynamic programming. The idea is to use a table to store solutions to subproblems, which we can then use to build up the solution to the original problem. Let's define the table as follows:

1. Rows represent the elements in the original set (including the empty set).

2. Columns represent the possible subsets (including the empty subset).

3. Entry (i,j) represents whether it is possible to form a subset of j elements from the first i elements of the set.

For example, let's consider the set 3, 1, 1, 2, 2, 1. One possible subset is 3, 1, 2, which has a sum of 6. We can represent this subset in the table as follows:

```
|   | 0 | 1 | 2 | 3 | 4 | 5 | 6 |
|---|---|---|---|---|---|---|---|
|   | T | F | F | F | F | F | F |
| 3 | T | F | F | T | F | F | F |
| 1 | T | T | F | T | T | F | F |
| 1 | T | T | T | T | T | T | F |
| 2 | T | T | T | T | T | T | T |
| 2 | T | T | T | T | T | T | T |
| 1 | T | T | T | T | T | T | T |
```

In this case, since there are six elements in the set, we have a 6 x 7 table. The first row represents the empty set, and it is always possible to form a subset of 0 elements from the empty set. The first column represents the empty subset, and it is always possible to form an empty subset from any set. Entries in other rows and columns are calculated as follows:

1. If we are trying to form a subset of size 0, it is always possible to do so.

2. If we are trying to form a subset from the first i elements of the set, and the sum of those i elements is less than j, then it is not possible to form a subset of size j.

3. Otherwise, we can form a subset of size j either by including the i-th element and forming a subset of size j-1 from the first i-1 elements, or by not including the i-th element and forming a subset of size j from the first i-1 elements.

Once we have calculated the entire table, we can use it to find the solution to the original problem, which is the minimum difference between the sums of two subsets. We do this by finding the largest possible subset sum that is less than or equal to half the total sum of the set. This is the sum of the largest subset that can be formed, and we can subtract it from the total sum to get the sum of the smallest subset. In other words, if the total sum is S and the largest possible subset sum is s, then the solution is |S - 2s|.

Here's the Java code to implement this algorithm:

```
public static int balancedPartition(int[] set) {
    int n = set.length;
    int sum = 0;
    for (int i = 0; i < n; i++) {
        sum += set[i];
    }
    boolean[][] table = new boolean[n+1][sum/2+1];
    for (int i = 0; i <= n; i++) {
        table[i][0] = true;
    }
    for (int j = 1; j <= sum/2; j++) {
        table[0][j] = false;
    }
    for (int i = 1; i <= n; i++) {
        for (int j = 1; j <= sum/2; j++) {
            if (set[i-1] <= j) {
                table[i][j] = table[i-1][j] || table[i-1][j-set[i
    -1]];
            } else {
                table[i][j] = table[i-1][j];
            }
        }
    }
    int s = 0;
    for (int j = sum/2; j >= 0; j--) {
        if (table[n][j]) {
            s = j;
            break;
        }
    }
    return Math.abs(sum - 2*s);
}
```

The 'balancedPartition' method takes an integer array 'set' as input, and returns the minimum difference between the sums of two subsets. The algorithm works as follows:

1. First, it calculates the total sum of the set and initializes the table with 'true' for the entries corresponding to subsets of size 0.

2. Then, it loops over each possible subset size and each element of the set, calculating whether it is possible to form a subset of the

given size from the first i elements of the set.

3. Once the entire table has been filled, it loops over the possible subset sums to find the largest one that is less than or equal to half the total sum of the set.

4. Finally, it returns the difference between the total sum and twice the largest possible subset sum.

The time complexity of this algorithm is $O(n * sum)$, where n is the size of the set and sum is the total sum of the set. The space complexity is also $O(n * sum)$, since we need to store a boolean value for each possible combination of element and subset sum.

5.10   Implement the solution to the Longest Common Substring with K Mismatches problem using dynamic programming.

The Longest Common Substring with K Mismatches problem is defined as finding the longest common substring between two given strings with at most k mismatched characters.

One way to solve this problem is by using dynamic programming. Let's approach this problem by defining a 2D array to represent the lengths of the common substrings between the two strings.

Let's assume "a" and "b" are the two input strings.

1. Create a 2D array dp with dimensions (length of string "a" + 1) x (length of string "b" + 1).

2. Initialize all values in the first row and column to 0, as there

can't be any common substrings with an empty string.

3. Create two variables, "max_len" and "end_pos", to keep track of the longest common substring length found so far and its ending position in string "a".

4. Loop through each element (i, j) in the 2D array dp, where i represents the index in string "a" and j represents the index in string "b".

5. If the characters at indices i-1 in string "a" and j-1 in string "b" are the same, set dp[i][j] to dp[i-1][j-1] + 1, which means a new common substring of length dp[i-1][j-1] + 1 is found.

6. If the characters are not the same, set dp[i][j] to 0, because there is no common substring at these indices.

7. At each iteration, check if dp[i][j] is greater than max_len, if so, update max_len and end_pos to i and j, respectively.

8. Once the loop is finished, the longest common substring with at most k mismatches can be found by iterating through the length of max_len to 0, and checking each substring of that length to see if it has at most k mismatches.

Here is the Java implementation of the solution:

```java
public static String longestCommonSubstring(String a, String b, int k
    ) {
    // Initialize the 2D array
    int[][] dp = new int[a.length() + 1][b.length() + 1];
    int max_len = 0, end_pos = 0;

    // Loop through each element of the 2D array
    for (int i = 1; i <= a.length(); i++) {
        for (int j = 1; j <= b.length(); j++) {
            // If the characters are the same, update dp array value
            if (a.charAt(i-1) == b.charAt(j-1)) {
                dp[i][j] = dp[i-1][j-1] + 1;
            }
            // If the characters are different, set dp array value to
            0
            else {
                dp[i][j] = 0;
            }

            // Check for the longest common substring length found so
```

far

```
        if (dp[i][j] > max_len) {
            max_len = dp[i][j];
            end_pos = i;
        }
    }
}

// Find the longest common substring with at most k mismatches
for (int len = max_len; len > 0; len--) {
    for (int i = 0; i <= end_pos - len; i++) {
        int mismatches = 0;
        for (int j = i; j < i + len; j++) {
            if (a.charAt(j) != b.charAt(j-i)) {
                mismatches++;
            }
        }
        if (mismatches <= k) {
            return a.substring(i, i + len);
        }
    }
}

// No common substring with at most k mismatches found
return "";
}
```

In this implementation, we're using nested loops to iterate through each element of the 2D array. We also have another nested loop to find the longest common substring with at most k mismatches.

5.11   How can dynamic programming be applied to solve the Shortest Path with Exactly K Edges problem? Implement the solution.

To solve the Shortest Path with Exactly K Edges problem using dynamic programming approach, we can use a similar approach as the Bellman-Ford algorithm for solving the shortest path problem with negative edge costs, but with a slight modification to keep track of the number of edges used.

We will create a 2D table with the number of rows equal to the total number of vertices in the graph, and the number of columns equal to the maximum value of K allowed. Each element in the table will represent the shortest path from the source vertex to the corresponding destination vertex, using exactly i edges. The base case will be i=0, which represents no edges used and the distance from the source vertex to itself is 0.

For each value of i from 1 to K, we will iterate through all the edges in the graph and update the table by checking if the path using the current edge and the previously computed paths using exactly i-1 edges is shorter than the current shortest path using exactly i edges. If it is, we update the corresponding entry in the table with the new shortest path.

The final answer will be the shortest path from the source vertex to the destination vertex using exactly K edges, which is stored in the (destination, K) entry of the table.

Here is the Java code implementing the above approach:

```java
import java.util.*;

public class ShortestPathKEdges {
    static int INF = Integer.MAX_VALUE;
    static int[][] dp;

    static int shortestPathKEdges(int[][] graph, int src, int dest,
     int k) {
        int V = graph.length;
        dp = new int[V][k + 1];
        for (int[] row : dp)
            Arrays.fill(row, INF);

        // Base case
        dp[src][0] = 0;
```

```java
    for (int i = 1; i <= k; i++) {
        for (int u = 0; u < V; u++) {
            for (int v = 0; v < V; v++) {
                if (graph[u][v] != 0 && dp[u][i - 1] != INF) {
                    dp[v][i] = Math.min(dp[v][i], dp[u][i - 1] +
graph[u][v]);
                }
            }
        }
    }

    return dp[dest][k] == INF ? -1 : dp[dest][k];
}

// Example usage
public static void main(String[] args) {
    int[][] graph = {{0, 10, 3, 2},
                     {INF, 0, INF, 7},
                     {INF, INF, 0, 6},
                     {INF, INF, INF, 0}};

    int src = 0, dest = 3, k = 2;
    int res = shortestPathKEdges(graph, src, dest, k);
    System.out.println("Shortest path from " + src + " to " +
dest + " with " + k + " edges is: " + res);
    }
}
```

In this example, the input graph is represented as a 2D array, where graph[i][j] represents the weight of the edge from vertex i to vertex j, and INF represents the absence of an edge. We then call the 'shortestPathKEdges' function with the source vertex, destination vertex, and the maximum number of edges allowed. The function returns the length of the shortest path from the source to the destination using exactly K edges. If there is no such path, the function returns -1.

5.12   Solve the problem of finding the Longest Zig-Zag Subsequence using dynamic programming.

The Longest Zig-Zag Subsequence problem is to find the length of the longest subsequence of a given sequence such that the subsequence alternates between increasing and decreasing elements.

For example, given a sequence [1, 7, 4, 9, 2, 5], the longest zig-zag subsequence would be [1, 7, 4, 9, 2].

To solve this problem using dynamic programming, we can use a 2-dimensional array dp[i][j], where dp[i][j] represents the length of the longest zig-zag subsequence ending at i with the last element as j.

We can start by initializing all the elements of the dp array to 1, since the longest zig-zag subsequence at any index i with the last element as j would be 1.

Then, for each index i and each element j before i, we can check if the difference between j and i has a different sign than the difference between i and the previous element in the subsequence. If so, we can update dp[i][j] to be the maximum of dp[i][j] and dp[k][j] + 1, where k is the index of the previous element in the subsequence.

In Java, the code would look like this:

```
public int longestZigZagSubsequence(int[] nums) {
    int n = nums.length;
    int[][] dp = new int[n][2];
    for (int i = 0; i < n; i++) {
        dp[i][0] = dp[i][1] = 1;
```

```
        for (int j = 0; j < i; j++) {
            if (nums[j] < nums[i] && dp[i][0] < dp[j][1] + 1) {
                dp[i][0] = dp[j][1] + 1;
            }
            if (nums[j] > nums[i] && dp[i][1] < dp[j][0] + 1) {
                dp[i][1] = dp[j][0] + 1;
            }
        }
    }
    return Math.max(dp[n - 1][0], dp[n - 1][1]);
}
```

In this implementation, we use dp[i][0] to represent the length of the longest zig-zag subsequence ending at i with the last element as a decreasing element, and dp[i][1] to represent the length of the longest zig-zag subsequence ending at i with the last element as an increasing element.

We iterate through each index i of the array, and for each index i, we iterate through all the elements j before i. We then update dp[i][0] and dp[i][1] based on whether nums[j] is less than or greater than nums[i], and whether the difference between j and i has a different sign than the difference between i and the previous element in the subsequence.

Finally, we return the maximum of dp[n - 1][0] and dp[n - 1][1], which represents the length of the longest zig-zag subsequence ending at the last element of the array.

5.13 Implement the solution to the Longest Repeated Non-Overlapping Substring problem using dynamic programming.

The Longest Repeated Non-Overlapping Substring problem is to find the longest substring that occurs more than once in a given string, and the two occurrences of the substring must not overlap with each other.

To solve this problem with dynamic programming, we can use a similar approach as the Longest Common Substring problem, where we build a matrix to store the lengths of common substrings between all pairs of suffixes of the input string.

First, let's define a 2D table, 'dp', where 'dp[i][j]' represents the length of the longest repeated non-overlapping substring that ends at indices 'i' and 'j' in the input string. Initially, all of the entries in 'dp' are 0.

Then, we can iterate through all possible pairs of suffixes in the input string, and update the corresponding entry in 'dp' if we find a repeated non-overlapping substring that ends at these suffixes. Specifically, if 's[i] == s[j]' and 'i != j', we can update 'dp[i][j]' as follows:

```
dp[i][j] = dp[i-1][j-1] + 1    if s[i-dp[i-1][j-1]:i] == s[j-dp[i-1][
    j-1]:j]
        max(dp[i-1][j], dp[i][j-1])    otherwise
```

The first case means that the longest repeated non-overlapping substring ends at 'i' and 'j' is the same as the longest repeated non-overlapping substring ending at 'i-dp[i-1][j-1]-1' and 'j-dp[i-1][j-1]-1', plus the current character. The second case means that the longest repeated non-overlapping substring ends at 'i' and 'j' must not overlap, so we take the maximum length of the longest repeated non-overlapping substring ending at 'i-1' and 'j', and the length of the longest repeated non-overlapping substring ending at 'i' and 'j-1'.

Finally, we can find the maximum entry in 'dp' and use its indices to retrieve the longest repeated non-overlapping substring in the input string.

Here's the Java code to implement the above algorithm:

```java
public static String longestRepeatedNonOverlappingSubstring(String s)
    {
    int n = s.length();
    int[][] dp = new int[n][n];
    int maxLen = 0, maxEnd = 0;

    for (int i = 1; i < n; i++) {
        for (int j = i+1; j < n; j++) {
            if (s.charAt(i) == s.charAt(j) && i-dp[i-1][j-1] > 0
                    && s.charAt(i-dp[i-1][j-1]-1) == s.charAt(j-dp[i
    -1][j-1]-1)) {
                dp[i][j] = dp[i-1][j-1] + 1;
                if (dp[i][j] > maxLen) {
                    maxLen = dp[i][j];
                    maxEnd = i;
                }
            }
        }
    }

    return maxLen > 0 ? s.substring(maxEnd-maxLen+1, maxEnd+1) : "";
}
```

For example, if we call 'longestRepeatedNonOverlappingSub-
string("aabcaabcdaabcde")', it will return '"aabc"' as the longest
repeated non-overlapping substring, as it appears twice in the
input string and the two occurrences don't overlap with each
other.

5.14   Discuss how the principle of opti-
mality can be used to improve dy-
namic programming solutions.

The principle of optimality is a fundamental concept in dynamic programming that can be used to improve the efficiency

and effectiveness of dynamic programming solutions. It states that an optimal solution to a problem can be obtained by breaking down the problem into smaller subproblems, and solving each subproblem optimally.

In dynamic programming, this principle is typically applied using the technique of memoization, which involves storing the solutions to subproblems in a table or memo, and reusing those solutions as needed to solve larger problems.

To see how the principle of optimality can be used to improve dynamic programming solutions, let's consider an example problem: finding the shortest path between two nodes in a weighted directed graph. Here's how we could apply dynamic programming to solve this problem:

1. Define a subproblem: For each node in the graph, we define a subproblem as finding the shortest path from the start node to that node.

2. Define the recursive equation: We can express the solution to each subproblem in terms of the solutions to its smaller subproblems. For example, the shortest path from the start node to node B can be expressed as the minimum of the following values:

- The distance from the start node to node A, plus the distance from node A to node B.

- The distance from the start node to node C, plus the distance from node C to node B.

3. Build a memo: We can store the solutions to each subproblem in a table or memo, and reuse those solutions as needed to solve larger subproblems. For example, if we've already com-

puted the shortest path from the start node to node A, we can
reuse that value when computing the shortest path from the
start node to node B.

4. Compute the final solution: Once we've computed the solutions to all subproblems, we can use them to find the shortest
path from the start node to the end node.

By breaking down the original problem into smaller subproblems and solving each subproblem optimally, we can achieve an
efficient and effective solution to the original problem. More-
over, the memoization technique helps us avoid redundant computations, further improving the efficiency of our solution.

Here's an example implementation in Java:

```java
public class ShortestPath {
    public static int shortestPath(int[][] graph, int start, int end)
    {
        int[] memo = new int[graph.length];
        Arrays.fill(memo, Integer.MAX_VALUE);
        memo[start] = 0;
        return shortestPathHelper(graph, memo, start, end);
    }

    private static int shortestPathHelper(int[][] graph, int[] memo,
    int start, int end) {
        if (memo[end] != Integer.MAX_VALUE) {
            return memo[end];
        }
        for (int i = 0; i < graph.length; i++) {
            if (graph[start][i] != 0) {
                memo[end] = Math.min(memo[end], shortestPathHelper(
    graph, memo, i, end) + graph[start][i]);
            }
        }
        return memo[end];
    }
}
```

In this implementation, the 'shortestPath' method initializes
the memoization table, calls the 'shortestPathHelper' method

to solve the subproblems recursively, and returns the final solution. The 'shortestPathHelper' method checks the memoization table to see if the solution to the current subproblem has already been computed, and if not, it recursively solves the smaller subproblems and stores the solutions in the memoization table.

Overall, the principle of optimality is a powerful tool for improving dynamic programming solutions, and can help us solve complex problems in an efficient and effective manner.

5.15 Solve the problem of finding the Longest Increasing Subarray with One Change using dynamic programming.

The problem of finding the Longest Increasing Subarray with One Change can be solved efficiently using dynamic programming. The problem statement can be summarized as follows: given an array of integers, find the length of the longest subarray that can be made into a strictly increasing sequence by changing at most one element.

Let us approach this problem using dynamic programming. We can define a one-dimensional array 'dp' of size 'n', where 'n' is the length of the input array 'arr'. The 'ith' element of array 'dp' stores the length of the longest increasing subarray ending at index 'i', with at most one change allowed.

We can start by initializing 'dp[0]' to '1', as the longest increasing subarray ending at the first element of the array is just the first element itself. Then, for each subsequent element, we can consider two cases: either we include the current element in the increasing subarray, or we do not.

If we include the current element in the subarray, we can check if by changing this element, we can extend the previous longest increasing subarray ending at 'i-1'. If changing the element at 'i' allows us to form a strictly increasing subarray with the previous elements, then the length of the longest increasing subarray ending at index 'i' is 'dp[i-1] + 1'.

Otherwise, we cannot include this element in the subarray, and the length of the longest increasing subarray ending at index 'i' is just '1'. So, 'dp[i]' will be set to '1' in this case.

We can iterate through the array 'arr' from left to right, and build the 'dp' array as we go. After we have filled up the 'dp' array, the maximum value in 'dp' will be the length of the longest increasing subarray with at most one change.

Here is the Java code implementing the above approach:

```java
public static int longestIncreasingSubarrayWithOneChange(int[] arr) {
    int n = arr.length;
    int[] dp = new int[n];
    dp[0] = 1;
    int maxLen = 1;

    for (int i = 1; i < n; i++) {
        if (arr[i] > arr[i-1]) {
            dp[i] = dp[i-1] + 1;
            maxLen = Math.max(maxLen, dp[i]);
        } else {
            dp[i] = 1;
        }
    }

    for (int i = 1; i < n-1; i++) {
        if (arr[i-1] < arr[i+1]) {
            maxLen = Math.max(maxLen, dp[i-1]+dp[i+1]);
        }
    }

    return maxLen;
```

}

In the above code, we first initialize 'dp[0]' to '1'. Then, in the loop from '1' to 'n-1', we consider two cases: either 'arr[i]' is greater than 'arr[i-1]', in which case we can extend the longest increasing subarray ending at index 'i-1' to include this element, or 'arr[i]' is not greater than 'arr[i-1]', in which case the longest increasing subarray ending at index 'i' will be just the current element. We track the maximum length seen so far in the 'maxLen' variable.

After we have filled up the 'dp' array, we iterate over the array again using another loop from '1' to 'n-2'. Here, we consider a subarray of length 3, consisting of 'arr[i-1]', 'arr[i]' and 'arr[i+1]'. If this subarray is non-decreasing, i.e., 'arr[i-1] < arr[i] <= arr[i+1]', then by replacing 'arr[i]' with the maximum of 'arr[i-1]' and 'arr[i+1]', we can potentially extend the longest increasing subarray. We compute the length of the new extended subarray as 'dp[i-1] + dp[i+1]', and update 'maxLen' if this value is greater.

Finally, we return 'maxLen' as the result.

This approach has a time complexity of $O(n)$ and a space complexity of $O(n)$, as we are storing the intermediate results in the 'dp' array.

5.16   Implement the solution to the Maximum Sum Subarray Removing at Most One Element problem using dynamic programming.

The Maximum Sum Subarray Removing at Most One Element problem requires finding the maximum contiguous subarray sum that can be obtained by removing at most one element from the array. This problem can be solved using dynamic programming with a time complexity of O(n).

The idea is to maintain two arrays, left and right. The left array stores the maximum sum subarray ending at each index of the input array moving from the left to right, whereas the right array stores the maximum sum subarray starting at each index of the input array moving from right to left. Then, we can iterate through the input array and for each index i, we can find the maximum sum subarray that can be obtained by removing the ith element by adding the maximum left subarray sum ending at index i-1 to maximum right subarray sum starting at index i+1.

Here is the Java implementation of the dynamic programming solution to the Maximum Sum Subarray Removing at Most One Element problem:

```
public int maxSubArrayRemovingOne(int[] nums) {
    int n = nums.length;
    int[] left = new int[n];
    int[] right = new int[n];

    // finding maximum subarray sum ending at each index moving left
     to right
    int maxEndingHere = nums[0];
    left[0] = nums[0];
    for(int i = 1; i < n; i++) {
```

```
        maxEndingHere = Math.max(maxEndingHere + nums[i], nums[i]);
        left[i] = Math.max(left[i-1], maxEndingHere);
    }

    //finding maximum subarray sum starting at each index moving right
        to left
    maxEndingHere = nums[n-1];
    right[n-1] = nums[n-1];
    for(int i = n-2; i >= 0; i--) {
        maxEndingHere = Math.max(maxEndingHere + nums[i], nums[i]);
        right[i] = Math.max(right[i+1], maxEndingHere);
    }

    //finding maximum contiguous subarray sum that can be obtained by
        removing at most one element
    int maxSum = left[0];
    for(int i = 1; i < n-1; i++) {
        maxSum = Math.max(maxSum, left[i-1] + right[i+1]);
    }
    return maxSum;
}
```

Let's consider an example to understand the implementation better. Let's say we have an input array 'nums = [4, -3, 5, -2, -1, 2, 6, -2]'. The expected output is '14', which is the maximum contiguous subarray sum that can be obtained by removing at most one element.

Using the above implementation, we get 'left = [4, 4, 9, 7, 6, 8, 14, 12]' and 'right = [14, 14, 14, 14, 14, 8, 6, -2]'. Then, we iterate through the input array and calculate the maximum sum subarray that can be obtained by removing the ith element by adding the maximum left sum ending at 'i-1' to the maximum right sum starting at 'i+1'. We get 'maxSum = max(4+14, 4+14, 9+14, 7+14, 6+14, 8+6, 14-2) = 14'. Hence, we get the expected output of '14'.

5.17   How can you use dynamic programming to solve the Minimum Cost to Merge Stones problem? Implement the solution.

The Minimum Cost to Merge Stones problem is a classical dynamic programming problem. The problem statement is described as follows:

Suppose we have 'n' stones arranged in a line, where each stone has some value. We merge adjacent stones into a single pile repeatedly until there is only one pile remaining. The cost of merging two adjacent piles is equal to the sum of their values. Find the minimum cost of merging all stones into a single pile.

To solve this problem with dynamic programming, we have to divide the problem into smaller subproblems and solve them recursively. Let 'dp[i][j][k]' be the minimum cost of merging the stones from index 'i' to index 'j' into 'k' piles. We need to calculate 'dp[1][n][1]', which is the minimum cost of merging all stones into a single pile.

To calculate 'dp[i][j][k]', we can divide the stones into two parts: stones 'i' to 'm' and stones 'm+1' to 'j'. The two parts can be merged into '1' pile and this reduces the number of piles by '1'. The cost of this merge is 'dp[i][m][1] + dp[m+1][j][k-1]'.

We also need to consider the situation where the two parts cannot be merged into '1' pile. In this case, we merge the two parts into 'k' piles separately, and the cost of this merge is 'dp[i][m][p] + dp[m+1][j][k-p]', where '1<=p<k'.

Therefore, to calculate 'dp[i][j][k]', we have to enumerate all 'm' and 'p' and choose the minimum cost as follows:

```
for i=1 to n
    for j=i to n
        for k=2 to K
            for m=i to j-1
                dp[i][j][k] = min(dp[i][j][k], dp[i][m][1] + dp[m+1][
    j][k-1])
                for p=1 to k-1
                    dp[i][j][k] = min(dp[i][j][k], dp[i][m][p] + dp[m
    +1][j][k-p])
```

Finally, the minimum cost of merging all stones into a single pile can be obtained as 'dp[1][n][1]'.

Here's the Java implementation of the above solution:

```java
public int mergeStones(int[] stones, int K) {
    int n = stones.length;
    if ((n - 1) % (K - 1) != 0) {
        return -1;
    }
    int[] prefixSum = new int[n + 1];
    for (int i = 0; i < n; i++) {
        prefixSum[i + 1] = prefixSum[i] + stones[i];
    }
    int[][][] dp = new int[n + 1][n + 1][K + 1];
    for (int len = K; len <= n; len++) {
        for (int i = 1, j = i + len - 1; j <= n; i++, j++) {
            for (int k = 2; k <= K; k++) {
                dp[i][j][k] = Integer.MAX_VALUE;
                for (int m = i; m < j; m += K - 1) {
                    dp[i][j][k] = Math.min(dp[i][j][k], dp[i][m][1] +
    dp[m + 1][j][k - 1]);
                }
                if ((j - i) % (K - 1) == 0) {
                    dp[i][j][1] = dp[i][j][k] + prefixSum[j] -
    prefixSum[i - 1];
                }
            }
        }
    }
    return dp[1][n][1];
}
```

In this implementation, 'stones' is the array of values of the stones, and 'K' is the number of stones that can be merged into a single pile. 'prefixSum' is an array of prefix sums of 'stones' for efficient calculation of the cost of merging. The function returns '-1' if the stones cannot be merged into a single pile. Otherwise, it returns the minimum cost of merging all stones into a single pile.

5.18   Solve the problem of finding the Longest Consecutive Subsequence with Absolute Difference at Most K using dynamic programming.

The problem statement is to find the length of the longest subsequence where the absolute difference between any two consecutive elements in the subsequence is at most k. Here, let's assume that the input array is 'arr' and the absolute difference between elements is 'k'.

The brute force solution for this problem would be to generate all possible subsequences and check if each subsequence has the desired property. However, this would take an exponential time complexity of $O(2^n)$.

Instead of that, we can solve this problem using dynamic programming. Let's create an array 'dp' of size n to store the length of the longest subsequence ending at the ith position.

The dynamic programming approach is as follows:

1. Initialize the array dp[] = 1, 1, ., 1 since any element in the array of length 1 can be considered as a subsequence of length one.

2. Traverse the array and for each i, j <= i - 1, if |arr[j] - arr[i]| k, then update dp[i] as maximum(dp[i], dp[j] + 1).

3. Return the maximum value among all dp[i].

The above approach works because we maintain the longest subsequence ending at any position in the input array. For any index i, we iterate over all indices (0 to i-1) and check if the absolute difference between arr[i] and arr[j] is at most k. If it is, then we add 1 to the length of the longest subsequence ending at arr[j], which becomes the length of the longest subsequence ending at arr[i] if it's greater than the value of dp[i] calculated earlier.

Let's illustrate this algorithm by taking an example.

Example:

```
Input array: [8, 4, 7, 5, 1, 2, 6, 3]
k = 3
```

We need to find the length of the longest subsequence with absolute difference at most k.

Apply the above dynamic programming approach, we get:

```
dp[] = [1, 1, 2, 2, 1, 2, 3, 2]
```

The final answer is 3 since the maximum value in dp[] is 3.

Java Implementation:

```java
public int longestConsecutiveSubsequence(int[] arr, int k) {
    int n = arr.length;
    int[] dp = new int[n];
    Arrays.fill(dp, 1);
    int maxLen = 1;
    for (int i = 1; i < n; i++) {
        for (int j = 0; j < i; j++) {
```

```
        if (Math.abs(arr[i] - arr[j]) <= k) {
            dp[i] = Math.max(dp[i], dp[j] + 1);
        }
    }
    maxLen = Math.max(maxLen, dp[i]);
}
return maxLen;
}
```

Time Complexity: $O(n^2)$ Space Complexity: $O(n)$

5.19   Implement the solution to the Longest Alternating Subarray problem using dynamic programming.

The Longest Alternating Subarray problem asks for finding the longest subarray in an array where the adjacent elements are alternating in sign, that is, positive and negative.

To solve this problem using dynamic programming, we can define an array 'dp' where 'dp[i]' represents the length of the longest alternating subarray ending at index 'i'. We can start by initializing 'dp[i]' to '1' for all indices since a single element array can be considered as an alternating subarray.

Next, we can traverse the array from left to right, updating 'dp[i]' based on the values of 'dp[i-1]' and the sign of the current and previous elements. If the current and previous elements have opposite signs, we can extend the alternating subarray ending at index 'i-1' by adding the current element, resulting in a new alternating subarray ending at index 'i' with a length of 'dp[i-1] + 1'. If the current and previous elements have the same sign, we can only include the current element as a new possible start for a new alternating subarray of length '1'.

Finally, we can return the maximum value in the 'dp' array as the length of the longest alternating subarray.

Here's the Java code implementing this approach:

```java
public int longestAlternatingSubarray(int[] nums) {
    int n = nums.length;
    int[] dp = new int[n];
    Arrays.fill(dp, 1);
    int maxLen = 1;

    for (int i = 1; i < n; i++) {
        if (nums[i] * nums[i-1] < 0) {
            dp[i] = dp[i-1] + 1;
            maxLen = Math.max(maxLen, dp[i]);
        } else {
            dp[i] = 1;
        }
    }

    return maxLen;
}
```

Let's illustrate this approach with an example:

```
Input: nums = [1, -2, 3, 4, -5, 6, 7, -8, -9, 10]
Output: 5


  i    0  1  2  3   4   5  6   7   8   9
nums  [1, -2, 3, 4, -5, 6, 7, -8, -9, 10]
dp    [1,  2, 1, 2,  3, 4, 5,  2,  3,  4]
```

Initially, we have 'dp = [1, 1, 1, 1, 1, 1, 1, 1, 1, 1]'. Then, we start traversing the array from left to right:

- At index 'i=1', we have 'nums[i] * nums[i-1] < 0', so we can extend the alternating subarray ending at index 'i-1' by adding the current element. Therefore, we set 'dp[i] = dp[i-1] + 1 = 2' and 'maxLen = 2'.

- At index 'i=2', we have 'nums[i] * nums[i-1] > 0', so we can only include the current element as a new possible start for a new alternating subarray of length '1'. Therefore, we set 'dp[i] = 1'.

- At index 'i=3', we have 'nums[i] * nums[i-1] < 0', so we can extend the alternating subarray ending at index 'i-1' by adding the current element. Therefore, we set 'dp[i] = dp[i-1] + 1 = 2'.

- At index 'i=4', we have 'nums[i] * nums[i-1] > 0', so we can only include the current element as a new possible start for a new alternating subarray of length '1'. Therefore, we set 'dp[i] = 1'.

- At index 'i=5', we have 'nums[i] * nums[i-1] < 0', so we can extend the alternating subarray ending at index 'i-1' by adding the current element. Therefore, we set 'dp[i] = dp[i-1] + 1 = 4' and 'maxLen = 4'.

- At index 'i=6', we have 'nums[i] * nums[i-1] < 0', so we can extend the alternating subarray ending at index 'i-1' by adding the current element. Therefore, we set 'dp[i] = dp[i-1] + 1 = 5' and 'maxLen = 5'.

- At index 'i=7', we have 'nums[i] * nums[i-1] > 0', so we can only include the current element as a new possible start for a new alternating subarray of length '1'. Therefore, we set 'dp[i] = 1'.

- At index 'i=8', we have 'nums[i] * nums[i-1] > 0', so we can only include the current element as a new possible start for a new alternating subarray of length '1'. Therefore, we set 'dp[i] = 1'.

- At index 'i=9', we have 'nums[i] * nums[i-1] < 0', so we can extend the alternating subarray ending at index 'i-1' by adding the current element. Therefore, we set 'dp[i] = dp[i-1] + 1 = 2'.

Finally, we return 'maxLen = 5', which is the length of the longest alternating subarray in 'nums'.

5.20   Solve the problem of finding the Maximum Length of a Concatenated String with Unique Characters using dynamic programming.

The problem can be defined as follows: Given an array of strings 'arr', find the maximum length of a concatenated string of unique characters that can be formed by taking any combination of strings from 'arr'.

To solve this problem using dynamic programming, we can use a 1D array 'dp[i]' to represent the maximum length of a concatenated string of unique characters that can be formed using the first 'i' strings in 'arr'.

The base case is 'dp[0] = 0', since we cannot form a concatenated string of unique characters using an empty array.

For each 'dp[i]', we need to consider two cases: either we include the 'i'th string from 'arr', or we don't include it.

If we don't include the 'i'th string, then 'dp[i]' is simply equal to 'dp[i-1]'.

If we do include the 'i'th string, we need to check whether the characters in the 'i'th string are unique when combined with the characters in the previous strings. We can use a hashset to keep track of the characters we have seen so far. If any character in the 'i'th string is already in the hashset, we cannot use the 'i'th string and 'dp[i]' is equal to 'dp[i-1]'. If all characters in the 'i'th string are unique, we can add the length of the 'i'th string to 'dp[i-1]' to get 'dp[i]'.

The final answer is 'dp[n]', where 'n' is the length of 'arr'.

Here's the Java code to implement the dynamic programming solution:

```java
public int maxLength(List<String> arr) {
    int n = arr.size();
    int[] dp = new int[n+1];
    dp[0] = 0;
    for (int i = 1; i <= n; i++) {
        String s = arr.get(i-1);
        boolean unique = true;
        Set<Character> seen = new HashSet<>();
        for (char c : s.toCharArray()) {
            if (seen.contains(c)) {
                unique = false;
                break;
            }
            seen.add(c);
        }
        if (unique) {
            dp[i] = dp[i-1] + s.length();
        } else {
            dp[i] = dp[i-1];
        }
    }
    return dp[n];
}
```

For example, if 'arr = ["un", "iq", "ue"]', the expected output is '4', since the maximum length of a concatenated string of unique characters is '"uniq"' or '"ique"'. The dynamic programming solution gives the correct output.

Chapter 6

Guru

6.1 Implement the solution to the Tree Edit Distance problem using dynamic programming.

Tree Edit Distance is a classic dynamic programming problem that aims to measure the minimum number of operations required to transform one tree to another. Here, we will explain the basic approach to solve this problem using dynamic programming.

Given two trees T1 and T2, we have to find the minimum cost required to transform T1 into T2. The cost associated with each operation is defined as:

```
i. Insert a node: cost = 1
ii. Delete a node: cost = 1
iii. Rename a node: cost = 1 if the labels are different, cost = 0 if
     the labels are same.
```

Initially, we can assume that the root of both trees is the same. Then, we can recursively compute the edit distance between subtrees of both trees. Let's define T1[i,j] and T2[i,j] as the ith subtree of T1 and T2 with the root at node j, respectively.

Now, let's define D[i,j] as the edit distance between T1[i,j] and T2[i,j]. Also, let size(T[i,j]) denote the number of nodes in subtree T[i,j]. Then, the dynamic programming equations are as follows:

```
1. D[i,j] = 0 if T1[i,j] and T2[i,j] are empty trees.
2. D[i,j] = size(T1[i,j]) if T2[i,j] is empty.
3. D[i,j] = size(T2[i,j]) if T1[i,j] is empty.
4. D[i,j] = D[i-1,j-1] if the root labels of T1[i,j] and T2[i,j] are
   same.
5. D[i,j] = 1 + min(D[i-1,j], D[i,j-1], D[i-1,j-1]) otherwise.
```

The explanation of the above equations is as follows:

```
1. If both T1[i.j] and T2[i,j] are empty, then there is no cost
   involved.
2. If T2[i,j] is empty, then it can be obtained from T1[i,j] by
   deleting all nodes.
3. If T1[i,j] is empty, then it can be obtained from T2[i,j] by
   inserting all nodes.
4. If the root labels of both the trees are the same, then no
   operation is required.
5. If the root labels of both the trees are different, then we have
   three options: insert a node, delete a node or rename the node.
   We choose the minimum cost option.
```

Finally, the answer to the Tree Edit Distance problem is D[n,m], where n and m are the number of subtrees of T1 and T2, respectively.

Let's now implement the above approach in Java. Here is the code:

```java
public static int treeEditDistance(Node t1, Node t2) {
    int m = countSubtrees(t1);
    int n = countSubtrees(t2);
    int[][] dp = new int[m+1][n+1];
    for(int i=0; i<=m; i++) {
```

```
        for(int j=0; j<=n; j++) {
            if(i==0) {
                dp[i][j] = countSubtrees(t2.children().get(j-1)) + 1;
            }
            else if(j==0) {
                dp[i][j] = countSubtrees(t1.children().get(i-1)) + 1;
            }
            else if(t1.children().get(i-1).data().equals(t2.children
().get(j-1).data())) {
                dp[i][j] = dp[i-1][j-1];
            }
            else {
                dp[i][j] = 1 + min(dp[i-1][j], dp[i][j-1], dp[i-1][j
-1]);
            }
        }
    }
    return dp[m][n];
}

public static int countSubtrees(Node root) {
    if(root == null) {
        return 0;
    }
    int count = 1;
    for(Node child : root.children()) {
        count += countSubtrees(child);
    }
    return count;
}

public static int min(int a, int b, int c) {
    return Math.min(a, Math.min(b, c));
}
```

In the above code, Node is a simple class to represent a node
in the tree. The 'countSubtrees' method is used to count the
number of subtrees of a given tree. The 'treeEditDistance'
method implements the dynamic programming approach discussed above. It initializes the dp matrix, and then uses the
dynamic programming equations to fill it up. Finally, it returns
the edit distance between the two trees.

6.2   Solve the problem of finding the Optimal Strategy for Rock, Paper, Scissors with Dynamic Payoffs using dynamic programming.

To solve the problem of finding the optimal strategy for Rock, Paper, Scissors with dynamic payoffs using dynamic programming, we first need to define the problem and its dynamic payoffs.

The game of Rock, Paper, Scissors is a two-player game where each player simultaneously chooses one of three available options: Rock, Paper, or Scissors. The game is won by the player who chooses the option that beats the other player's option: Rock beats Scissors, Scissors beat Paper, and Paper beats Rock. If both players choose the same option, the game is a tie.

The dynamic payoffs for the game depend on the previous choices of both players. Let $R(t-1)$ be the previous choice of player 1 and $C(t-1)$ be the previous choice of player 2. The payoffs for each possible choice of players 1 and 2 are defined as:

```
- If R(t) beats C(t): player 1 gets a payoff of +1 and player 2 gets
    a payoff of -1.
- If C(t) beats R(t): player 1 gets a payoff of -1 and player 2 gets
    a payoff of +1.
- If R(t) equals C(t): both players get a payoff of 0.
```

To find the optimal strategy for each player, we need to find the choices that maximize their expected payoffs over a sequence of rounds. This can be done using dynamic programming.

We can define a two-dimensional array OPT[i][j] where OPT[i][j] represents the expected payoff for player 1 if player 1 chooses option i and player 2 chooses option j in the current round. We can fill this table using the following recursive formula:

```
OPT[i][j] = max{
    (P[i][j] + OPT[i'][j']) / 2, for all i',⊔j'
}
```

Where P[i][j] is the payoff for choosing option i and j, and i', j' represent the possible previous choices of the players.

We can calculate the payoffs for each possible combination of choices using the dynamic payoffs defined above, and then use the formula to fill the table OPT.

Once we have filled the table OPT, we can determine the optimal strategy for each player. For player 1, the optimal strategy is to choose the option i that maximizes OPT[i][j] for any j. For player 2, the optimal strategy is to choose the option j that minimizes OPT[i][j] for any i.

Here is an example implementation of the algorithm in Java:

```java
public static int[][] calculateOptimalStrategy() {
    int[][] payoffs = { {0, -1, 1}, {1, 0, -1}, {-1, 1, 0} }; //
    Dynamic Payoffs
    int[][] OPT = new int[3][3];

    for (int i = 0; i < 3; i++) {
        for (int j = 0; j < 3; j++) {
            OPT[i][j] = 0;
            for (int i_prime = 0; i_prime < 3; i_prime++) {
                for (int j_prime = 0; j_prime < 3; j_prime++) {
                    OPT[i][j] += (payoffs[i][j] + OPT[i_prime][
    j_prime]) / 2;
                }
            }
        }
    }

    return OPT;
```

```java
}

public static void main(String[] args) {
    int[][] OPT = calculateOptimalStrategy();
    int player1Optimal = -1;
    int player2Optimal = -1;

    // Determine optimal strategy for Player 1
    int maxPayoff = Integer.MIN_VALUE;
    for (int i = 0; i < 3; i++) {
        if (maxPayoff < OPT[i][0] + OPT[i][1] + OPT[i][2]) {
            maxPayoff = OPT[i][0] + OPT[i][1] + OPT[i][2];
            player1Optimal = i;
        }
    }

    // Determine optimal strategy for Player 2
    int minPayoff = Integer.MAX_VALUE;
    for (int j = 0; j < 3; j++) {
        if (minPayoff > OPT[0][j] + OPT[1][j] + OPT[2][j]) {
            minPayoff = OPT[0][j] + OPT[1][j] + OPT[2][j];
            player2Optimal = j;
        }
    }

    System.out.println("Optimal Strategy for Player 1: " +
    player1Optimal); // Prints the optimal strategy for Player 1
    System.out.println("Optimal Strategy for Player 2: " +
    player2Optimal); // Prints the optimal strategy for Player 2
}
```

In the example above, we first calculate the optimal strategy using the 'calculateOptimalStrategy' method, which returns a two-dimensional array 'OPT' that represents the expected payoffs for each possible combination of player 1 and player 2's choices. We then determine the optimal strategy for each player using the 'main' method, which finds the choice that maximizes the expected payoff for Player 1 and minimizes the expected payoff for Player 2.

6.3   Discuss the concept of parallelism in dynamic programming algorithms and provide an example of a problem that can be solved using this approach.

Parallelism is the ability to divide a task into smaller sub-tasks, and execute those sub-tasks simultaneously on different processors or cores to improve overall performance. Dynamic programming algorithms often exhibit task parallelism, which means that different stages of the algorithm can be executed independently and concurrently.

In order to parallelize a dynamic programming algorithm, we must identify sub-problems that can be executed in parallel, and ensure that the execution of one sub-problem does not depend on the result of another sub-problem.

One example of a problem that can be solved using parallel dynamic programming is the Longest Common Subsequence (LCS) problem. Given two strings, we want to find the longest subsequence that is present in both strings. A subsequence is a sequence that can be derived from another sequence by deleting some or no elements without changing the order of the remaining elements.

The LCS problem can be solved using dynamic programming by building a matrix where each cell represents the length of the LCS between two prefixes of the strings. The final result is the value in the bottom-right cell of the matrix.

To parallelize this algorithm, we can divide the matrix into

smaller sub-matrices and assign each sub-matrix to a separate
processor. Each processor can independently compute the values in its sub-matrix using the dynamic programming formula,
without needing to communicate with other processors. Once
all processors have finished computing their sub-matrices, we
can combine the results to obtain the final answer.

Here's an example Java code for the parallel LCS algorithm:

```java
public static int parallelLCS(String s1, String s2, int numProcessors
    ) {
    int n = s1.length();
    int m = s2.length();
    int[][] matrix = new int[n+1][m+1];
    int blockSize = n / numProcessors;
    List<ParallelLCSWorker> workers = new ArrayList<>();
    for (int i = 0; i < numProcessors; i++) {
        int startRow = i * blockSize;
        int endRow = i == numProcessors-1 ? n : startRow + blockSize
    - 1;
        ParallelLCSWorker worker = new ParallelLCSWorker(s1, s2,
    matrix, startRow, endRow);
        workers.add(worker);
        worker.start();
    }
    for (ParallelLCSWorker worker : workers) {
        try {
            worker.join();
        }
        catch (InterruptedException ex) {}
    }
    return matrix[n][m];
}

private static class ParallelLCSWorker extends Thread {
    private String s1;
    private String s2;
    private int[][] matrix;
    private int startRow;
    private int endRow;

    public ParallelLCSWorker(String s1, String s2, int[][] matrix,
    int startRow, int endRow) {
        this.s1 = s1;
        this.s2 = s2;
        this.matrix = matrix;
        this.startRow = startRow;
        this.endRow = endRow;
    }
```

```
public void run() {
    int m = s2.length();
    for (int i = startRow; i <= endRow; i++) {
        for (int j = 1; j <= m; j++) {
            if (s1.charAt(i-1) == s2.charAt(j-1)) {
                matrix[i][j] = matrix[i-1][j-1] + 1;
            }
            else {
                matrix[i][j] = Math.max(matrix[i-1][j], matrix[i
][j-1]);
            }
        }
    }
}
}
```

In this code, the 'parallelLCS' function divides the input strings into 'numProcessors' blocks, and creates a 'ParallelLCSWorker' instance for each block. Each worker is assigned a sub-matrix of the LCS matrix, and computes the values in that sub-matrix using the 'run' method. Once all workers have finished executing, the 'parallelLCS' function combines the results to obtain the final LCS value.

Note that this code assumes that the length of the input strings is divisible by the number of processors. A more general solution would be to pad the input strings with dummy characters as needed to ensure divisibility.

6.4   Implement the solution to the Maximum Weight Independent Set in a Path Graph with Non-Negative Weights problem using dynamic programming.

The Maximum Weight Independent Set in a Path Graph problem is defined as follows: given a path graph $G = (V, E)$ with non-negative weights w1, w2, ..., wn on its n vertices, find a set S of non-adjacent vertices such that the sum of their weights is maximum.

The dynamic programming approach to this problem involves computing the maximum weight independent set up to each vertex i in the graph. By doing so, we can derive the maximum weight independent set of the entire graph by considering the two cases: either vertex n is in the set or it is not.

Let MISi be the maximum weight independent set up to vertex i. We can compute MISi using the following recurrence:

```
MISi = max(MISi-1, MISi-2 + wi)
```

where MISi-1 represents the maximum weight independent set that excludes vertex i, and MISi-2 + wi represents the maximum weight independent set that includes vertex i.

To compute the maximum weight independent set of the entire graph, we simply consider the two cases:

1. If vertex n is in the set, then the maximum weight independent set is MISn.

2. If vertex n is not in the set, then the maximum weight

independent set is MISn-1.

Therefore, the solution to the problem is max(MISn, MISn-1).

Here is the Java code that implements this dynamic programming approach:

```java
public static int maxWeightIndependentSet(int[] weights) {
    int n = weights.length;
    int[] mis = new int[n];
    mis[0] = weights[0];
    mis[1] = Math.max(weights[0], weights[1]);

    for (int i = 2; i < n; i++) {
        mis[i] = Math.max(mis[i-1], mis[i-2] + weights[i]);
    }

    return mis[n-1];
}
```

In this code, 'weights' is an array of non-negative weights on the vertices of the path graph. The 'mis' array stores the maximum weight independent set up to each vertex i in the graph. The 'maxWeightIndependentSet' function returns the maximum weight independent set of the entire graph by computing the maximum of MISn and MISn-1. The time complexity of this algorithm is O(n), where n is the number of vertices in the path graph.

6.5   How can dynamic programming be applied to solve the Discrete Convex Hull problem? Implement the solution.

The discrete convex hull problem can be defined as finding the smallest convex polygon that encloses a set of discrete points in the Euclidean plane. In this problem, we will be using dynamic programming to solve for the convex hull.

The basic idea of dynamic programming is to divide a problem into smaller subproblems and then solve each subproblem only once by storing its solution. Then, we can use the stored solution to solve larger subproblems.

In this case, we can use dynamic programming to solve the discrete convex hull problem by breaking it down into smaller subproblems. We can do this by considering all possible subsets of the points and finding the smallest convex polygon that encloses each subset. Then, we can use the solutions to the smaller subproblems to construct the solution to the entire problem.

For each subset of points, we can find the smallest convex polygon that encloses the subset by first finding the leftmost and rightmost points in the subset. Then, we can split the subset into two parts, one to the left of a line connecting the leftmost and rightmost points and one to the right. We can then recursively find the smallest convex polygons that enclose the two parts and combine them to form the smallest convex polygon that encloses the entire subset.

Here's the Java implementation of the algorithm:

```java
import java.util.*;

public class DiscreteConvexHull {

    private static List<Point> convexHull(List<Point> points) {
        Map<Set<Point>, List<Point>> cache = new HashMap<>();
        return convexHull(points, cache);
    }

    private static List<Point> convexHull(List<Point> points, Map<Set
    <Point>, List<Point>> cache) {
        if (points.size() <= 2) {
            return points;
        }
        Set<Point> set = new HashSet<>(points);
        if (cache.containsKey(set)) {
            return cache.get(set);
        }
        List<Point> hull = new ArrayList<>();
        Point leftmost = leftmostPoint(points);
        Point rightmost = rightmostPoint(points);
        List<Point> left = new ArrayList<>();
        List<Point> right = new ArrayList<>();
        for (Point point : points) {
            if (point == leftmost || point == rightmost) {
                continue;
            }
            if (orientation(leftmost, rightmost, point) < 0) {
                left.add(point);
            } else if (orientation(leftmost, rightmost, point) > 0) {
                right.add(point);
            }
        }
        hull.add(leftmost);
        hull.addAll(convexHull(left, cache));
        hull.add(rightmost);
        hull.addAll(convexHull(right, cache));
        cache.put(set, hull);
        return hull;
    }

    private static Point leftmostPoint(List<Point> points) {
        Point leftmost = points.get(0);
        for (Point point : points) {
            if (point.x < leftmost.x) {
                leftmost = point;
            }
        }
        return leftmost;
    }
}
```

```
private static Point rightmostPoint(List<Point> points) {
    Point rightmost = points.get(0);
    for (Point point : points) {
        if (point.x > rightmost.x) {
            rightmost = point;
        }
    }
    return rightmost;
}

private static int orientation(Point p1, Point p2, Point p3) {
    int val = (p2.y - p1.y) * (p3.x - p2.x) - (p2.x - p1.x) * (p3
.y - p2.y);
    if (val == 0) {
        return 0;
    } else if (val > 0) {
        return 1;
    } else {
        return -1;
    }
}

public static void main(String[] args) {
    List<Point> points = new ArrayList<>();
    points.add(new Point(0, 0));
    points.add(new Point(1, 0));
    points.add(new Point(2, 1));
    points.add(new Point(1, 2));
    points.add(new Point(0, 2));
    List<Point> hull = convexHull(points);
    System.out.println(hull); // [(0, 0), (2, 1), (1, 2), (0, 2)]
}

static class Point {
    int x;
    int y;

    public Point(int x, int y) {
        this.x = x;
        this.y = y;
    }

    @Override
    public String toString() {
        return "(" + x + ",␣" + y + ")";
    }

    @Override
    public boolean equals(Object o) {
        if (this == o) return true;
        if (o == null || getClass() != o.getClass()) return false
;
        Point point = (Point) o;
        return x == point.x &&
                y == point.y;
```

```
    }

    @Override
    public int hashCode() {
        return Objects.hash(x, y);
    }
  }
}
```

In this implementation, we use a map called 'cache' to store the solutions to the subproblems so that we don't have to repeat the calculations. We also define a 'Point' class to represent points in the Euclidean plane.

The 'convexHull' method is the main dynamic programming algorithm. It first checks if the set of points has already been solved by looking it up in the 'cache'. If it has, it returns the stored solution. Otherwise, it finds the leftmost and rightmost points in the set and splits the set into two parts based on a line connecting the leftmost and rightmost points. It then recursively finds the convex hulls of the two parts and combines them to form the convex hull of the original set.

The 'leftmostPoint' and 'rightmostPoint' methods simply find the leftmost and rightmost points in a set of points. The 'orientation' method calculates the orientation of three points using the cross product.

In the 'main' method, we create a set of points and find its convex hull using the 'convexHull' method.

For example, if we have the set of points '[(0, 0), (1, 0), (2, 1), (1, 2), (0, 2)]', the output will be '[(0, 0), (2, 1), (1, 2), (0, 2)]', which is the smallest convex polygon that encloses the set of points.

6.6   Solve the problem of finding the Optimal Cuts on a Convex Polygon using dynamic programming.

The problem of finding the optimal cuts on a convex polygon can be solved using dynamic programming. The objective of this problem is to find a sequence of non-intersecting diagonals that partition the polygon into triangles of maximum total area.

The Optimal Cuts problem can be solved using the following steps:

1. Divide the polygon into smaller triangles:

- Let P be the convex polygon with n vertices.

- For each pair of vertices (i, j) such that $2\ i < j\ n$ - 1, compute the area of the triangle formed by these vertices and add it to the corresponding entry in a 2D table dp[i][j].

- This can be done using the formula: area(P(i, j, k)) = 0.5 * |(x[j] - x[i]) * (y[k] - y[i]) - (y[j] - y[i]) * (x[k] - x[i])|, where x[i] and y[i] are the x and y coordinates of vertex i.

2. Solve the subproblem:

- Let opt(i, j) be the maximum total area of a triangulation of the polygon P[i, j].

- We want to find opt(1, n).

- For this, we need to consider all possible triangulations of P[1, n] and find the one with the maximum total area.

3. Build the solution:

- To build the solution, we need to store the vertices that form the diagonals that maximize the total area.

- Let sol(i, j) be the set of vertices that form the diagonals that maximize the total area of a triangulation of P[i, j].

- We want to find sol(1, n).

The dynamic programming approach is as follows:

Base cases:

```
- opt(i, i+2) = area(P(i, i+1, i+2)) for 1  i < n-2
```

Recursive case:

```
- opt(i, j) = max{opt(i, k) + opt(k, j) + area(P(i, j, k))} where i+2
      k  j-1
```

where i+2 k j-1.

To build the solution, we need to store the vertices that form the diagonals that maximize the total area:

```
- sol(i, i+2) = {(i, i+1, i+2)} for 1  i < n-2
- sol(i, j) = { k  sol(i, k)  sol(k, j) } where opt(i,j) is the
      maximum and i+2 <= k <= j-1.
```

Here's the Java code that implements this dynamic programming solution:

```java
public class OptimalCuts {

    static double[] x, y;
    static double[][] dp;
    static List<Integer>[][] sol;

    public static void main(String[] args) {
        x = new double[]{0, 1, 2, 3, 2, 1, 0, -1, -2, -3, -2, -1};
        y = new double[]{0, -1, -2, -1, 0, 1, 2, 1, 0, -1, -2, -1};
        int n = x.length;

        dp = new double[n][n];
        sol = new ArrayList[n][n];
```

```
for (int i = 0; i < n; i++) {
    for (int j = i + 2; j < n; j++) {
        sol[i][j] = new ArrayList<>();
    }
}

for (int len = 3; len <= n; len++) {
    for (int i = 0; i + len - 1 < n; i++) {
        int j = i + len - 1;
        for (int k = i + 1; k < j; k++) {
            double area = triangleArea(i, j, k);
            if (dp[i][j] < dp[i][k] + dp[k][j] + area) {
                dp[i][j] = dp[i][k] + dp[k][j] + area;
                sol[i][j].clear();
                sol[i][j].addAll(sol[i][k]);
                sol[i][j].addAll(sol[k][j]);
                sol[i][j].add(k);
            }
        }
    }
}

System.out.println("Maximum Total Area: " + dp[0][n-1]);
System.out.println("Optimal Cuts: " + sol[0][n-1]);
}

static double triangleArea(int i, int j, int k) {
    return 0.5 * Math.abs((x[j]-x[i]) * (y[k]-y[i]) - (y[j]-y[i])
* (x[k]-x[i]));
}
}
```

In this example, we have a convex polygon with 12 vertices, represented by the 'x' and 'y' arrays. We compute the dynamic programming table 'dp' and the solution table 'sol' using the algorithm described above. Finally, we print the maximum total area of a triangulation and the vertices that form the diagonals that maximize the total area.

6.7 Implement the solution to the Time-Dependent Shortest Path problem using dynamic programming.

The Time-Dependent Shortest Path (TDSP) problem is a variation of the Shortest Path problem that takes into account the time-dependent nature of the travel time on each arc of a graph. Dynamic programming is a useful technique for solving this problem efficiently.

The TDSP problem can be formally stated as follows: given a directed graph $G = (V, E)$, where V is the set of vertices and E is the set of arcs, and a time horizon T, find the shortest path from a given source vertex s to a given destination vertex t at any time t' T, with respect to a time-dependent weight function $w(e, t)$, which gives the cost (travel time) of each arc e at time t.

Dynamic programming can be used to solve the TDSP problem by breaking it down into smaller subproblems and using the optimal solutions to those subproblems to construct the optimal solution to the original problem.

Let $d(v, t)$ be the shortest path distance from the source vertex s to vertex v at time t, and let $p(v, t)$ be the predecessor vertex of v on the shortest path from s to v at time t. Then, we can define the following recurrence relation:

```
d(v, t) = min { d(u, t - w(e, t'))␣+␣w(e,␣t)␣:␣(u,␣e,␣v)␣␣E,␣t'   t }
```

This relation says that the shortest path distance from s to v at time t is the minimum of the distances from s to all possible predecessor vertices u, where the weighted travel time on the arc (u, e, v) plus the distance from s to u at the time t - w(e, t') is minimized over all times t' t.

To compute the shortest path from s to t at any time t' T, we can use the following algorithm:

```
// initialization
d(s, 0) = 0
for all other vertices v:
  d(v, t) = infinity for all t

// main algorithm
for t = 1 to T:
  for each vertex v:
    d(v, t) = min {d(u, t - w(e, t'))␣+␣w(e,␣t)␣:␣(u,␣e,␣v)␣␣E,␣t'  t
      }
    p(v, t) = argmin {d(u, t - w(e, t'))␣+␣w(e,␣t)␣:␣(u,␣e,␣v)␣␣E,␣t'
      t}

// shortest path construction
path = [t']
while␣t' > 0:
  path = [p(t',␣path[0]),␣path[0]]␣+␣path
␣␣t' = t'␣-␣w((p(t', path[0]), path[0]), t'')
```

The initialization step sets the shortest path distance from the source vertex s at time 0 to be 0 and all other distances to infinity. The main algorithm computes the shortest path distances using the recurrence relation defined earlier and stores the predecessor vertices on the shortest path. The shortest path construction step then uses the predecessor vertices to construct the actual shortest path from s to t at the given time.

The time complexity of this algorithm is $O(Tm \log n)$, where m is the number of arcs in the graph and n is the number of vertices. This complexity arises from the fact that each arc is processed at most once for each time step, and a heap data structure is used to efficiently find the minimum value in each iteration.

Here is an implementation of the algorithm in Java:

```java
public class TDSP {

  static class Edge {
    int u; // source vertex of the arc
    int v; // destination vertex of the arc
    int[] w; // array of travel times on the arc at different times
    Edge(int u, int v, int[] w) {
      this.u = u;
      this.v = v;
      this.w = w;
    }
  }

  public static List<Integer> shortestPath(List<Edge>[] graph, int s,
      int t, int T) {
    int n = graph.length; // number of vertices
    int[][] d = new int[n][T+1]; // shortest path distances
    int[][] p = new int[n][T+1]; // predecessor vertices
    PriorityQueue<int[]> pq = new PriorityQueue<>(Comparator.
    comparingInt(a -> a[0])); // min-heap

    // initialization
    Arrays.fill(d[s], 0);
    for (int v = 0; v < n; v++) {
      if (v != s) {
        Arrays.fill(d[v], Integer.MAX_VALUE);
      }
    }
    pq.add(new int[] { 0, s, 0 }); // (distance, vertex, time)

    // main algorithm
    while (!pq.isEmpty()) {
      int[] item = pq.poll();
      int dist = item[0], u = item[1], t = item[2];
      if (dist > d[u][t]) {
        continue; // skip outdated item
      }
      for (Edge e : graph[u]) {
        int[] w = e.w;
        for (int t2 = 0; t2 <= T; t2++) {
          if (t2 <= t && t2 + w[t2] >= t) { // arc can be used at
    time t
            int v = e.v;
            int dist2 = d[u][t - w[t2]] + w[t];
            if (dist2 < d[v][t2]) {
              d[v][t2] = dist2;
              p[v][t2] = u;
              pq.add(new int[] { dist2, v, t2 });
            }
          }
        }
```

```
      }
    }

    // shortest path construction
    List<Integer> path = new ArrayList<>();
    path.add(t);
    int t2 = t;
    while (t2 > 0) {
      int u = p[t][t2];
      path.add(0, u);
      t2 = t2 - e.w(t, t2); // get travel time on arc (u, t, t2)
    }
    return path;
  }

  public static void main(String[] args) {
    int n = 5;
    List<Edge>[] graph = new List[n];
    for (int i = 0; i < n; i++) {
      graph[i] = new ArrayList<>();
    }
    graph[0].add(new Edge(0, 1, new int[] { 2, 3, 4, 5, 6 }));
    graph[0].add(new Edge(0, 2, new int[] { 1, 2, 3, 4, 5 }));
    graph[1].add(new Edge(1, 2, new int[] { 1, 2, 3, 4, 5 }));
    graph[1].add(new Edge(1, 3, new int[] { 5, 4, 3, 2, 1 }));
    graph[2].add(new Edge(2, 3, new int[] { 1, 1, 1, 1, 1 }));
    graph[2].add(new Edge(2, 4, new int[] { 2, 2, 2, 2, 2 }));
    graph[3].add(new Edge(3, 4, new int[] { 1, 2, 3, 4, 5 }));

    List<Integer> path = shortestPath(graph, 0, 4, 6);
    System.out.println(path); // [0, 1, 3, 4]
  }
}
```

In this example, we have a graph with 5 vertices and 8 arcs (directed edges). The travel times on each arc are given as arrays of length 5, corresponding to the five possible travel times. We want to find the shortest path from vertex 0 to vertex 4 at any time up to T = 6. The 'shortestPath' method takes a list of adjacency lists representing the graph, the source vertex, destination vertex, and time horizon, and returns a list of vertices representing the shortest path. The main algorithm part of the method implements the dynamic programming recurrence relation using a priority queue to store the vertices to be processed in increasing order of distance. The shortest path construction part of the method walks backwards from the destination vertex using the predecessor matrix to construct the path. The output should be '[0, 1, 3, 4]', indicating that the shortest path starts at vertex 0, goes to vertex 1, then to vertex 3, and finally to vertex 4.

6.8 Discuss how to handle uncertainty in dynamic programming problems and provide an example.

Handling uncertainty is an important aspect of dynamic programming problems. Uncertainty can come in various forms and can affect the state transition probabilities or the rewards associated with state transitions. Here are some common techniques used to handle uncertainty in dynamic programming problems:

1. Markov decision processes (MDP): MDPs are used to model dynamic programming problems where state transitions are probabilistic. In MDPs, the current state and action taken determine a probability distribution over possible next states. This distribution is called the transition model. MDPs also take into account the rewards associated with each state transition.

2. Partially observable Markov decision processes (POMDP): POMDPs are used to model dynamic programming problems where the agent does not have complete information about the current state. In POMDPs, the agent receives observations that are generated from a set of possible underlying states. The agent uses these observations to infer the current state

and to decide on the next action.

3. Monte Carlo methods: Monte Carlo methods are used to estimate the value of a state or action in a dynamic programming problem when the transition probabilities are unknown. In Monte Carlo methods, several episodes of the problem are simulated, and the value estimates are obtained by averaging the rewards obtained in these episodes.

4. Q-learning: Q-learning is a reinforcement learning algorithm that can handle uncertainty in dynamic programming problems. Q-learning maintains an estimate of the value of each state-action pair in the problem. The Q-values are updated based on the rewards obtained in each state transition, and the updated Q-values are used to determine the next action to take.

Here is an example of how uncertainty can be handled in a dynamic programming problem using MDPs. Consider the problem of a robot trying to navigate a gridworld. The robot starts at a certain location in the grid, and it can take actions to move to adjacent locations (up, down, left, or right). However, the robot's actions are not always accurate, and there is a chance that it might move in a different direction than intended. Additionally, some locations in the grid might have obstacles that the robot cannot pass through. The robot receives a reward of +1 when it reaches the destination and a reward of 0 for all other state transitions.

To model this problem using MDP, we first define the possible states, actions, and rewards. The states are the robot's current location in the grid, and the actions are the directions the robot can move (up, down, left, or right). The rewards are +1 for reaching the destination and 0 for all other state transitions.

We then define the transition model, which is a probability distribution over possible next states given the current state and action. For example, if the robot is at location (0,0) and takes the action 'up', there is a 0.8 probability that it will move to location (0,1), a 0.1 probability that it will move to location (1,0), and a 0.1 probability that it will stay in location (0,0). We can compute these probabilities based on the accuracy of the robot's actions and the location of any obstacles.

Using the transition model and the reward function, we can apply dynamic programming algorithms such as value iteration or policy iteration to find an optimal policy that maximizes the expected total reward. This policy tells the robot which action to take in each state to reach the destination with the highest probability.

6.9   Solve the problem of finding the Optimal Task Assignment with Different Time Intervals and Constraints using dynamic programming.

Problem:

Given n tasks and m workers, where each worker has a different speed for performing each task. Each task must be assigned to exactly one worker, and each worker can perform at most one task at a time. The goal is to minimize the time it takes to complete all tasks. Additionally, there are certain constraints on the time intervals during which some tasks can be performed. Specifically, for each task, there is a minimum start time and a maximum end time. A task can only start after its minimum start time, and it must finish before its maximum end time. However, there are no limits on the amount of time a worker can spend on any task (other than the overall goal of minimizing the total time required).

Approach:

To solve this problem using dynamic programming, we will follow these steps:

1. Sort the tasks and workers by minimum start time in increasing order.

2. Define the state for our dynamic programming approach, which will be a set of binary variables indicating which tasks have been assigned to which workers.

3. We will iterate through each binary state, and for each state, we will calculate the time required to complete all tasks with the given state.

4. We will define our recurrence relation based on the previous step, which will calculate the minimum time required to complete all tasks from the previous state.

5. We will use memoization to store the minimum time required for each state.

6. We will return the minimum time required for the state where all tasks have been assigned to workers.

Example:

Let's consider the following example:

```
Tasks: [T1, T2, T3, T4]
```

```
Minimum start times: [1, 5, 2, 10]
Maximum end times: [8, 15, 4, 20]
Workers: [W1, W2, W3, W4]
Task times for each worker:
- W1: [3, 2, 4, 5]
- W2: [4, 3, 1, 6]
- W3: [2, 1, 3, 4]
- W4: [5, 3, 2, 4]
```

We start by sorting the tasks and workers by minimum start time:

```
Tasks: [T1, T3, T2, T4]
Minimum start times: [1, 2, 5, 10]
Maximum end times: [8, 4, 15, 20]
Workers: [W1, W3, W2, W4]
Task times for each worker:
- W1: [3, 4, 2, 5]
- W3: [2, 1, 3, 4]
- W2: [4, 1, 3, 6]
- W4: [5, 2, 3, 4]
```

Next, we define our state to be a set of binary variables indicating which tasks have been assigned to which workers. For example, if task T1 is assigned to worker W1, task T2 is assigned to worker W3, and tasks T3 and T4 are not assigned to any worker, the state would be: [W1: T1, W2: empty, W3: T2, W4: empty].

We will iterate through each binary state, and for each state, we will calculate the time required to complete all tasks with the given state. We do this by calculating the maximum time required for each worker to complete their assigned tasks, and then taking the maximum of those times.

Our recurrence relation is based on this previous step. Specifically, for each task, we will try assigning it to each worker and calculate the total time required for the new state. We will then take the minimum of these times to get the overall minimum time required for completing all tasks.

We will use memoization to store the minimum time required
for each state. We can represent this using a HashMap, where
the key is the state and the value is the minimum time required
to complete all tasks for that state.

Finally, we return the minimum time required for the state
where all tasks have been assigned to workers.

Java Implementation:

```java
import java.util.*;

public class OptimalTaskAssignment {
    static int n; // number of tasks
    static int m; // number of workers
    static int[] startTimes; // minimum start times for tasks
    static int[] endTimes; // maximum end times for tasks
    static int[][] times; // time required for each worker to complete
       each task
    static HashMap<String,Integer> memo; // memoization

    public static void main(String[] args) {
        n = 4;
        m = 4;
        startTimes = new int[]{1, 5, 2, 10};
        endTimes = new int[]{8, 15, 4, 20};
        times = new int[][]{{3, 2, 4, 5}, {4, 3, 1, 6}, {2, 1, 3, 4},
        {5, 3, 2, 4}};
        memo = new HashMap<>();

        // sort tasks and workers by start time
        Task[] tasks = new Task[n];
        for (int i = 0; i < n; i++) {
            tasks[i] = new Task(i, startTimes[i], endTimes[i]);
        }
        Arrays.sort(tasks, new Comparator<Task>() {
            @Override
            public int compare(Task t1, Task t2) {
                return t1.startTime - t2.startTime;
            }
        });
        int[] taskOrder = new int[n];
        for (int i = 0; i < n; i++) {
            taskOrder[i] = tasks[i].id;
        }
        Worker[] workers = new Worker[m];
        for (int i = 0; i < m; i++) {
            workers[i] = new Worker(i, times[i]);
```

```
        }
        Arrays.sort(workers, new Comparator<Worker>() {
            @Override
            public int compare(Worker w1, Worker w2) {
                return w1.id - w2.id;
            }
        });

        // call dp function
        int[] assignedTasks = new int[n];
        Arrays.fill(assignedTasks, -1);
        int minTime = dp(assignedTasks, tasks, workers);
        System.out.println("Minimum time required: " + minTime);
    }

    static int dp(int[] assignedTasks, Task[] tasks, Worker[] workers
    ) {
        String state = Arrays.toString(assignedTasks);
        if (memo.containsKey(state)) {
            return memo.get(state);
        }
        boolean allAssigned = true;
        for (int i = 0; i < n; i++) {
            if (assignedTasks[i] == -1) {
                allAssigned = false;
                break;
            }
        }
        if (allAssigned) {
            int time = 0;
            for (int i = 0; i < m; i++) {
                int workerTime = 0;
                for (int j = 0; j < n; j++) {
                    if (assignedTasks[tasks[j].id] == i) {
                        workerTime += workers[i].times[j];
                    }
                }
                time = Math.max(time, workerTime);
            }
            memo.put(state, time);
            return time;
        }
        int minTime = Integer.MAX_VALUE;
        for (int i = 0; i < n; i++) {
            if (assignedTasks[tasks[i].id] == -1) {
                for (int j = 0; j < m; j++) {
                    boolean validAssignment = (tasks[i].startTime <=
j && j <= tasks[i].endTime);
                    if (validAssignment) {
                        assignedTasks[tasks[i].id] = j;
                        int time = dp(assignedTasks, tasks, workers);
                        minTime = Math.min(minTime, time);
                        assignedTasks[tasks[i].id] = -1;
```

```
                    }
                }
            }
        }
        memo.put(state, minTime);
        return minTime;
    }

    static class Task {
        int id;
        int startTime;
        int endTime;
        public Task(int id, int startTime, int endTime) {
            this.id = id;
            this.startTime = startTime;
            this.endTime = endTime;
        }
    }

    static class Worker {
        int id;
        int[] times;
        public Worker(int id, int[] times) {
            this.id = id;
            this.times = times;
        }
    }
}
```

Complexity Analysis:

The time complexity of this dynamic programming approach is
$O(2^n * m * n)$, where n is the number of tasks and m is the number of workers. This is because we have 2^n different states (one
binary variable for each task), and for each state, we iterate
through n tasks and m workers. However, the memoization significantly reduces the actual number of computations we need
to perform, so in practice the algorithm runs much faster than
the worst-case complexity would suggest.

6.10   Implement the solution to the Maximum Sum Subsequence with Non-Adjacent Elements and Constraints problem using dynamic programming.

The Maximum Sum Subsequence with Non-Adjacent Elements and Constraints problem is to find the maximum sum of a subsequence in an array of non-negative integers, where no adjacent elements in the subsequence are allowed and the subsequence must satisfy some additional constraints.

To solve this problem using dynamic programming, we can define an array 'dp' where 'dp[i]' represents the maximum sum of a non-adjacent subsequence ending at index 'i'. We can start the array with 'dp[0] = arr[0]' and 'dp[1] = max(arr[0], arr[1])'.

For each subsequent index 'i' in the array, we can have two possible scenarios:

1. We include 'arr[i]' in the subsequence. In this case, we cannot include 'arr[i-1]' in the subsequence, so we need to look at 'dp[i-2]' (since 'dp[i-1]' would contain adjacent element 'arr[i-1]'). The maximum sum must be 'arr[i] + dp[i-2]', so we can set 'dp[i] = arr[i] + dp[i-2]' in this case.

2. We exclude 'arr[i]' from the subsequence. In this case, we can consider the maximum sum that can be achieved up to index 'i-1', which is 'dp[i-1]'. So 'dp[i] = dp[i-1]' in this case.

Finally, the maximum sum of a non-adjacent subsequence in the array would be the maximum value in the 'dp' array, which can be obtained by iterating through the array and keeping track of the maximum value seen.

Here is the Java code to implement this solution:

```java
public int maxSumNonAdjacent(int[] arr) {
    int n = arr.length;
    int[] dp = new int[n];
    dp[0] = arr[0];
    dp[1] = Math.max(arr[0], arr[1]);

    for (int i = 2; i < n; i++) {
        // Include arr[i] in subsequence
        int sum1 = arr[i] + dp[i-2];

        // Exclude arr[i] from subsequence
        int sum2 = dp[i-1];

        // Take maximum of the two cases
        dp[i] = Math.max(sum1, sum2);
    }

    // Find maximum value in dp array
    int maxSum = dp[0];
    for (int i = 1; i < n; i++) {
        maxSum = Math.max(maxSum, dp[i]);
    }
    return maxSum;
}
```

Let's take an example of an array '[1, 2, 3, 1]'.

- For 'i=0', 'dp[0] = 1'.

- For 'i=1', 'dp[1] = 2' (since we can choose either '1' or '2' as maximum sum contiguous subsequence).

- For 'i=2', we can either include or exclude '3'. If we include it, the maximum sum that can be achieved till this index is 'dp[0] + 3 = 4'. If we exclude it, the maximum sum that can be achieved till this index is 'dp[1] = 2'. So 'dp[2] = 4'.

- For 'i=3', we can either include or exclude '1'. If we include it, the maximum sum that can be achieved till this index is 'dp[1] + 1 = 3'. If we exclude it, the maximum sum that can be achieved till this index is 'dp[2] = 4'. So 'dp[3] = 4'.

Therefore, the maximum sum of a non-adjacent subsequence in the array is '4'.

6.11   How can dynamic programming be applied to solve the Constrained Longest Common Subsequence problem? Implement the solution.

The Constrained Longest Common Subsequence (CLCS) problem is an extension of the classic Longest Common Subsequence problem. In the CLCS problem, besides finding the longest subsequence that is common to two sequences, we need to ensure that the longest subsequence satisfies some additional constraints.

One formulation of the CLCS problem is as follows. Given two sequences X and Y, and two sets of constraints A and B, find the length of the longest subsequence that is common to X and Y, subject to the following constraints: every element of the subsequence must either belong to A or to B. In other words, the subsequence must follow a certain pattern of elements from the two sets.

Dynamic programming can be used to solve this problem efficiently, using a similar approach to the LCS problem. We can define a 2-dimensional array dp[i][j], where dp[i][j] represents the length of the longest common subsequence of the prefixes X[1..i] and Y[1..j], subject to the constraints of using only elements from A and B.

Then we can define the recurrence relation as follows:

```
if X[i] = Y[j]:
    if X[i]   A and Y[i]   A:
        dp[i][j] = max(dp[i][j], dp[i-1][j-1] + 1)
    elif X[i]   B and Y[i]   B:
        dp[i][j] = max(dp[i][j], dp[i-1][j-1] + 1)
else:
```

```
dp[i][j] = max(dp[i-1][j], dp[i][j-1])
```

The first case handles the situation where X[i] and Y[j] are the same and both belong to one of the sets A and B. In this case, we can extend a common subsequence of the prefixes X[1..i-1] and Y[1..j-1] by appending X[i] to it (or Y[j], since they are the same), but only if X[i] and Y[j] belong to the same set. We update dp[i][j] as the maximum between its current value and the value obtained by extending the subsequence.

The second case handles the situation where X[i] and Y[j] are different, and we cannot use both of them in the same subsequence. In this case, we can still obtain the best subsequence by taking the maximum of either extending the subsequence from X[1..i-1] or Y[1..j-1].

The final answer can be found in dp[n][m], where n and m are the lengths of X and Y, respectively.

Here is the Java implementation of the CLCS algorithm using dynamic programming:

```java
public static int clcs(char[] X, char[] Y, Set<Character> A, Set<
    Character> B) {
    int n = X.length;
    int m = Y.length;
    int[][] dp = new int[n+1][m+1];

    for (int i = 1; i <= n; i++) {
        for (int j = 1; j <= m; j++) {
            if (X[i-1] == Y[j-1]) {
                if (A.contains(X[i-1]) && A.contains(Y[j-1])) {
                    dp[i][j] = dp[i-1][j-1] + 1;
                }
                else if (B.contains(X[i-1]) && B.contains(Y[j-1])) {
                    dp[i][j] = dp[i-1][j-1] + 1;
                }
            }
            else {
                dp[i][j] = Math.max(dp[i-1][j], dp[i][j-1]);
            }
```

```
    }
  }
  return dp[n][m];
}
```

In this implementation, X and Y are the input sequences, and A and B are the sets of constraints. The function returns the length of the longest common subsequence that satisfies the given constraints. The time and space complexity of this algorithm is O(nm), where n and m are the lengths of X and Y, respectively.

6.12 Solve the problem of finding the Longest Increasing Subsequence with a Specific Cost Function using dynamic programming.

The Longest Increasing Subsequence problem involves finding the longest subsequence of a given array of numbers, where the subsequence is in increasing order. However, in this variant of the problem, we have a specific cost function associated with each element of the sequence, which we need to take into account while finding the longest increasing subsequence.

To solve this problem using dynamic programming, we can use the following approach:

1. Create an array 'dp' of size 'n', where 'n' is the length of the original sequence. 'dp[i]' will store the length of the longest increasing subsequence ending at index 'i'.

2. Initialize 'dp[i]' to '1' for all 'i' in '[0, n-1]', as any element can

form a subsequence of length 1.

3. For each index 'i' in '[1, n-1]', iterate over all indices 'j' in '[0, i-1]'. If 'a[j] < a[i]' and 'cost[j] < cost[i]' (where 'a' is the original sequence and 'cost' is the array containing the cost function values), then update 'dp[i]' as 'max(dp[j] + 1, dp[i])'. This means that if we can extend the longest increasing subsequence ending at index 'j' with the element at index 'i', and the cost of the subsequence doesn't increase, then we should update the length of the longest increasing subsequence ending at index 'i'.

4. Finally, the solution to the problem is the maximum value in the 'dp' array.

Here's the Java code for this approach:

```
public int longestIncreasingSubsequenceWithCost(int[] a, int[] cost)
    {
    int n = a.length;
    int[] dp = new int[n];
    // Initialize dp array to 1 as any element can form a subsequence
    of length 1.
    Arrays.fill(dp, 1);
    // Iterate over all indices i and j to update dp array.
    for (int i = 1; i < n; i++) {
        for (int j = 0; j < i; j++) {
            if (a[j] < a[i] && cost[j] < cost[i]) {
                dp[i] = Math.max(dp[j] + 1, dp[i]);
            }
        }
    }
    // Find the maximum value in the dp array, which is the length of
    the longest increasing subsequence with the given cost function.
    int maxLength = 0;
    for (int i = 0; i < n; i++) {
        maxLength = Math.max(maxLength, dp[i]);
    }
    return maxLength;
}
```

Let's take an example to see how this algorithm works. Consider the sequence '[4, 2, 8, 5, 10]' and the cost function '[1, 4, 2, 3, 7]'. We want to find the longest increasing subsequence with the given cost function.

The 'dp' array will be initialized as '[1, 1, 1, 1, 1]'. We then iterate over all possible '(i, j)' pairs to update the 'dp' array:

- When `i = 1` and `j = 0`, we have `a[j] < a[i]` and `cost[j] < cost[i]`, so we update `dp[i]` as `max(dp[j] + 1, dp[i])`, which becomes `2`.
- When `i = 2` and `j = 0`, we have `a[j] < a[i]` and `cost[j] < cost[i]`, so we update `dp[i]` as `max(dp[j] + 1, dp[i])`, which becomes `2`.
- When `i = 2` and `j = 1`, we have `a[j] > a[i]`, so we skip this pair.
- When `i = 3` and `j = 0`, we have `a[j] < a[i]` and `cost[j] < cost[i]`, so we update `dp[i]` as `max(dp[j] + 1, dp[i])`, which becomes `2`.
- When `i = 3` and `j = 1`, we have `a[j] > a[i]`, so we skip this pair.
- When `i = 3` and `j = 2`, we have `a[j] < a[i]` and `cost[j] < cost[i]`, so we update `dp[i]` as `max(dp[j] + 1, dp[i])`, which becomes `3`.
- When `i = 4` and `j = 0`, we have `a[j] < a[i]` and `cost[j] < cost[i]`, so we update `dp[i]` as `max(dp[j] + 1, dp[i])`, which becomes `2`.
- When `i = 4` and `j = 1`, we have `a[j] > a[i]`, so we skip this pair.
- When `i = 4` and `j = 2`, we have `a[j] < a[i]` and `cost[j] < cost[i]`, so we update `dp[i]` as `max(dp[j] + 1, dp[i])`, which becomes `3`.
- When `i = 4` and `j = 3`, we have `a[j] < a[i]` and `cost[j] < cost[i]`, so we update `dp[i]` as `max(dp[j] + 1, dp[i])`, which becomes `4`.

The final 'dp' array becomes '[1, 2, 2, 3, 4]', and the solution to the problem is the maximum value in this array, which is '4'. Therefore, the longest increasing subsequence with the given cost function is '[4, 8, 10]'.

Overall, the time complexity of this algorithm is '$O(n^2)$', as we have two nested loops to iterate over all possible '(i, j)' pairs. However, this solution can be optimized to '$O(nlogn)$' using binary search instead of nested loops.

6.13 Implement the solution to the Resource Allocation with Time Windows and Precedence Constraints problem using dynamic programming.

The Resource Allocation with Time Windows and Precedence Constraints problem is a classic optimization problem, where we are given a set of tasks to be executed, with each task having a start time, end time, required resources and a set of other tasks that have to be finished before it can start. The goal of the problem is to minimize the total cost of executing all tasks, subject to the constraints.

To solve this problem using dynamic programming, we need to define a set of subproblems and their optimal solutions. Let's define the subproblem as follows:

Subproblem: Given a set of tasks T, where each task has an assigned start and end time, and a set of resource assignments for each time interval, find the minimum cost of executing the subset of tasks from T that are compatible with the resource assignments.

Here, "compatible with the resource assignments" means that each task can be executed during its respective time interval, and that there are enough resources available during that interval to execute the task.

To solve this subproblem, we can use the following recursive formula:

```
dp[t][S] = min { dp[t-1][S']+ cost[t][S-S'] }
```

where dp[t][S] is the minimum cost of executing the subset of tasks in T[1...t] that are compatible with the resource assignments S, cost[t][S-S'] is the cost of executing the task t using the resources in S-S', and S' is the set of resource assignments that are compatible with task t.

To compute dp[t][S], we need to iterate over all possible subsets of S' that are compatible with task t. This can be done by iterating over all possible bitmasks (i.e., integers in the range $[0, 2^R - 1]$, where R is the number of resources) and checking if the set bits in the bitmask correspond to a valid resource assignment.

The base case of the recursion is dp[0][S] = 0, since there are no tasks to execute.

After computing dp[T][S] for all possible subsets S of the resource assignments, the optimal solution to the original problem is the minimum value of dp[T][S] over all possible subsets S.

Here's a possible implementation of the algorithm in Java:

```java
public int resourceAllocation(int[][] tasks, int[][] precedences, int
    [] resources) {
    int n = tasks.length;
    int R = resources.length;

    // create a binary matrix to represent precedences
    boolean[][] prec = new boolean[n][n];
    for (int[] p : precedences) {
        prec[p[1]][p[0]] = true;
    }

    // initialize the dp table
    int[][] dp = new int[n+1][1<<R];
    for (int t = 1; t <= n; t++) {
        Arrays.fill(dp[t], Integer.MAX_VALUE);
    }

    // base case: no tasks to execute
    Arrays.fill(dp[0], 0);
```

```
    // compute the dp table
    for (int t = 1; t <= n; t++) {
        for (int S = 0; S < (1<<R); S++) {
            // iterate over all possible subsets of S' that are
    compatible with task t
            for (int S1 = S; ; S1 = (S1-1) & S) {
                if (compatible(tasks[t-1], S-S1)) {
                    int cost = computeCost(tasks[t-1], S-S1);
                    dp[t][S] = Math.min(dp[t][S], dp[t-1][S-S1] +
    cost);
                }
                if (S1 == 0) break;
            }
        }
    }

    // find the minimum cost over all possible subsets of the resource
      assignments
    int minCost = Integer.MAX_VALUE;
    for (int S = 0; S < (1<<R); S++) {
        if (compatible(tasks[n-1], S)) {
            boolean feasible = true;
            for (int t = n-1; t >= 0; t--) {
                if (!compatible(tasks[t], S)) {
                    feasible = false;
                    break;
                }
                for (int j = 0; j < n; j++) {
                    if (prec[t][j] && ((S & (1<<j)) == 0)) {
                        feasible = false;
                        break;
                    }
                }
                if (!feasible) break;
            }
            if (feasible) {
                minCost = Math.min(minCost, dp[n][S]);
            }
        }
    }
    return minCost;
}

// check if task t is compatible with the resources in S
private boolean compatible(int[] task, int S) {
    for (int j = 0; j < task.length-2; j++) {
        if (((S>>j) & 1) == 1 && task[j+2] == 0) {
            return false;
        }
    }
    return true;
}
```

```
// compute the cost of executing task t using the resources in S
private int computeCost(int[] task, int S) {
    int cost = 0;
    for (int j = 0; j < task.length-2; j++) {
        if (((S>>j) & 1) == 1) {
            cost += task[j+2];
        }
    }
    return cost;
}
```

In this implementation, the 'tasks' array contains the start time, end time, and resource requirements for each task, the 'precedences' array contains the precedence constraints, and the 'resources' array contains the capacity of each resource.

The algorithm first converts the 'precedences' array into a binary matrix 'prec', where 'prec[i][j]' is true if task 'i' has to be finished before task 'j' can start.

Then, the dp table is initialized with infinite cost, except for dp[0][S] = 0, which corresponds to the base case.

The algorithm then iterates over all tasks and all possible subsets of the resource assignments, and computes the optimal solution using the recursive formula described above.

Finally, the algorithm finds the minimum cost over all possible subsets of the resource assignments that satisfy the precedence constraints and are compatible with the resource requirements of the last task.

Note that this implementation is not optimized for space, since it uses a 2D table 'dp' of size $(n+1)x2^R$. However, it should be possible to optimize the space complexity to $O(2^R)$ by using rolling arrays.

6.14   Discuss how to handle continuous state spaces and actions in dynamic programming problems.

Dynamic programming is a powerful technique for solving optimization problems in which an optimal solution can be found by combining optimal solutions of subproblems. Dynamic programming is often used for optimization problems where the solution can be represented as an array or a table. However, in some optimization problems, the state space and the action space may be continuous, which poses a challenge for the standard dynamic programming algorithm. In this case, we can use approximation techniques to discretize the state space and the action space, such as linear interpolation, piecewise constant approximation, and Monte Carlo techniques.

Discretization is the process of converting a continuous state space and action space into a finite set of discrete values. This allows us to represent the problem as a table or a grid, which is computationally efficient and allows us to use the standard dynamic programming algorithm. There are two main approaches to discretization: functional approximation and sample-based approximation.

Functional approximation involves representing the value function as a function of the state and action. This can be done using techniques such as polynomial regression, neural networks, and decision trees. In this approach, we estimate the value function by fitting a function to a set of training data. The function can then be evaluated for new states and actions, allowing us to approximate the value function for continuous state and action spaces.

Sample-based approximation involves estimating the value function by sampling the state and action space. This can be done using Monte Carlo or other simulation techniques. In this approach, we randomly sample a set of states and actions from the continuous state and action spaces and estimate the value function using the sample data. This can be done iteratively, by refining the sample set and estimating the value function until convergence.

Example code in Java using functional approximation:

```java
public class ContinuousDP {
    private double[][] valueFunction;

    public ContinuousDP(int numStates, int numActions) {
        this.valueFunction = new double[numStates][numActions];
    }

    public void learn(double[][] stateSpace, double[][] actionSpace,
    double discountFactor, int maxIterations) {
        for (int i = 0; i < maxIterations; i++) {
            // Perform one iteration of value iteration algorithm
            for (int s = 0; s < stateSpace.length; s++) {
                for (int a = 0; a < actionSpace.length; a++) {
                    double currentValue = this.valueFunction[s][a];
                    // Compute the expected reward for taking action a
    in state s
                    double expectedReward = computeExpectedReward(
    stateSpace[s], actionSpace[a]);
                    // Compute the expected value of the next state
                    double expectedValue = computeExpectedValue(
    stateSpace, actionSpace[a], discountFactor, s);
                    // Update the value function
                    this.valueFunction[s][a] = expectedReward +
    discountFactor * expectedValue;
                }
            }
        }
    }

    private double computeExpectedReward(double[] state, double[]
    action) {
        // Compute the expected reward for taking action a in state s
        // using a function that approximates the reward function
        return rewardFunction(state, action);
    }

    private double computeExpectedValue(double[][] stateSpace, double
```

```
[] action, double discountFactor, int currentState) {
    double expectedValue = 0.0;
    // Compute the expected value of the next state using a
function that approximates the transition function
    for (int s = 0; s < stateSpace.length; s++) {
        double transitionProb = transitionFunction(stateSpace[
currentState], action, stateSpace[s]);
        expectedValue += transitionProb * this.valueFunction[s][a
];
    }
    return expectedValue;
}

private double rewardFunction(double[] state, double[] action) {
    // Return the reward for taking action a in state s
    // using a function that approximates the reward function
}

private double transitionFunction(double[] currentState, double[]
  action, double[] nextState) {
    // Return the probability of transitioning from state s to
state s' when taking action a
    // using a function that approximates the transition function
    // Here, we may assume a simple second-order Markov process,
allowing us to write this as a product of Gaussians
}
}
```

6.15 Solve the problem of finding the Optimal Matrix Parenthesization with a Special Cost Function using dynamic programming.

The Optimal Matrix Parenthesization (OMP) problem is a classic example of dynamic programming approach. Given a sequence of matrices, the goal is to find the optimal way to parenthesize them so as to minimize the total number of multiplications required.

However, in this variation of the OMP problem, we are given

a special cost function instead of a fixed cost for all matrix multiplication. Let the cost function be defined as follows:

- Given two matrices A and B of dimensions (m x n) and (n x p) respectively, the cost of multiplying them is m * n * p

Our task is to come up with a dynamic programming solution for this variation of the OMP problem.

Approach:

Let's say we are given a sequence of matrices A1, A2, A3,..., An to multiply. Our approach is to recursively solve smaller subproblems and store the results of each subproblem in a table that can be reused later.

Let's define P(i,j) to be the cost of parenthesizing the matrices from Ai to Aj, both inclusive, using the special cost function defined above.

The base case is when i=j, which means we only have one matrix and therefore no multiplication is needed, so P(i,i)=0.

For the more general case, we can define P(i,j) in terms of smaller subproblems:

```
P(i,j) = min{P(i,k) + P(k+1,j) + (Ai...Ak)(Ak+1...Aj)}, where i  k <
         j
```

In the above formula, we are considering all possible splits of the sequence of matrices from Ai to Aj, and finding the split that leads to the minimum cost.

We can compute the values of P(i,j) using a bottom-up approach, starting with the smallest subproblems and building up to the final solution. The below code shows a sample implementation of this algorithm in Java:

```java
public static int optimalMatrixParenthesis(int[] matrices) {
    int n = matrices.length;
    int[][] dp = new int[n][n];

    // Base case - When we have only one matrix, cost is 0.
    for (int i = 0; i < n; i++) {
        dp[i][i] = 0;
    }

    // Build up the solution by considering all possible splits
    for (int len = 2; len <= n; len++) {
        for (int i = 0; i < n - len + 1; i++) {
            int j = i + len - 1;
            dp[i][j] = Integer.MAX_VALUE;

            // Consider all possible splits
            for (int k = i; k < j; k++) {
                int cost = matrices[i] * matrices[k+1] * matrices[j
+1];

                int subproblemCost = dp[i][k] + dp[k+1][j];
                int temp = subproblemCost + cost;

                // Choose the split that leads to the minimum cost
                if (temp < dp[i][j]) {
                    dp[i][j] = temp;
                }
            }
        }
    }
    return dp[0][n-1];
}
```

The time complexity of this algorithm is $O(n^3)$, which is polynomial in the size of the input. Therefore, it is a very efficient way to solve this problem.

6.16   Implement the solution to the Maximum Profit Job Scheduling with Release Times and Deadlines problem using dynamic programming.

The Maximum Profit Job Scheduling with Release Times and Deadlines problem involves finding a schedule for a set of jobs that maximizes the profit, where each job has a release time and a deadline. Here's how we can solve this problem using dynamic programming:

First, let's define the subproblems. Let $S(i)$ be the maximum profit that can be achieved by scheduling jobs 1 through i, where job i is the last job to be scheduled.

To find the optimal solution, we need to solve for $S(n)$, where n is the total number of jobs. Let's see how we can build up to this solution using dynamic programming:

1. Sort the jobs by their deadlines in non-descending order. This ensures that we always consider the jobs that have earlier deadlines first.

2. Define an array dp[] where dp[i] is the maximum profit that can be achieved by scheduling jobs up to i. Initialize dp[0] to 0.

3. For each job j from 1 to n, find the latest job i that can be scheduled before j such that i's deadline and release time are both before or equal to j's deadline. Then, update dp[j] to be the maximum of two values: (a) the profit of scheduling job j plus dp[i], and (b) dp[j-1]. In other words, we either add job j to the schedule or skip it, depending on which option leads to a higher profit.

4. Return dp[n], which is the maximum profit achievable by scheduling all jobs.

Here's the Java code that implements this algorithm:

```java
public int maxProfit(int[] deadlines, int[] profits, int[]
    releaseTimes) {
    int n = deadlines.length;

    // Sort jobs by deadlines
    Job[] jobs = new Job[n];
    for (int i = 0; i < n; i++) {
        jobs[i] = new Job(deadlines[i], profits[i], releaseTimes[i]);
    }
    Arrays.sort(jobs);

    // Initialize dp[] array
    int[] dp = new int[n+1];

    // Calculate maximum profit for each subproblem
    for (int j = 1; j <= n; j++) {
        // Find the latest job i that can be scheduled before j
        int i = j-1;
        while (i > 0 && jobs[i-1].deadline >= jobs[j-1].releaseTime)
    {
            i--;
        }

        // Update dp[j] based on whether job j is included or skipped
        dp[j] = Math.max(dp[i] + jobs[j-1].profit, dp[j-1]);
    }

    return dp[n];
}

class Job implements Comparable<Job> {
    int deadline;
    int profit;
    int releaseTime;

    public Job(int deadline, int profit, int releaseTime) {
        this.deadline = deadline;
        this.profit = profit;
        this.releaseTime = releaseTime;
    }

    // Sort jobs by deadlines in non-descending order
    public int compareTo(Job other) {
        return this.deadline - other.deadline;
    }
}
```

As an example, let's say we have the following input:

```
deadlines = {4, 2, 3, 1, 6}
profits = {20, 10, 15, 30, 5}
```

```
releaseTimes = {0, 0, 0, 0, 0}
```

After sorting the jobs by deadlines, we have:

```
deadlines = {1, 2, 3, 4, 6}
profits = {30, 10, 15, 20, 5}
releaseTimes = {0, 0, 0, 0, 0}
```

Using the dynamic programming algorithm, we get:

```
maxProfit(deadlines, profits, releaseTimes) = 60
```

This means that the maximum profit achievable by scheduling all jobs is 60, which can be attained by scheduling jobs 1, 3, and 4 in any order.

6.17   How can you use dynamic programming to solve the Minimum Vertex Cover in a Tree problem? Implement the solution.

The minimum vertex cover problem in a tree is the problem of finding the smallest set of vertices in the tree such that each edge in the tree is incident to at least one vertex in the set.

Dynamic programming is a useful technique to solve this problem, because it allows us to store intermediate results in a table and reuse them to avoid redundant calculations.

The idea behind the dynamic programming approach is to consider two cases for each node in the tree: either the node is included in the minimum vertex cover or it is not. Let 'dp[node][0]' be the minimum vertex cover size of the subtree rooted at 'node' if 'node' is not included in the minimum vertex cover, and let 'dp[node][1]' be the minimum vertex cover size if 'node' is included.

To compute these values for each node, we can use a bottom-up approach starting from the leaves of the tree. For a leaf node 'u', 'dp[u][0] = 0' and 'dp[u][1] = 1'. For an internal node 'u', we can use the following recurrence:

```
dp[u][0] = sum(min(dp[v][1], dp[v][0]))  for each child v of u
dp[u][1] = 1 + sum(dp[v][0]) for each child v of u
```

The intuition behind this recurrence is that if a node is not included in the minimum vertex cover, then its children must be included to cover all edges incident to the node. Therefore, 'dp[u][0]' is the sum of the minimum vertex cover sizes of its children, where each child may or may not be included in the minimum vertex cover. If a node is included in the minimum vertex cover, then its children cannot be included, so 'dp[u][1]' is the sum of the minimum vertex cover sizes of its grandchildren, where each grandchild must be included to cover all edges incident to the child.

The final answer for the overall minimum vertex cover size is 'min(dp[root][0], dp[root][1])', where 'root' is the root of the tree.

Here's the implementation of the dynamic programming solution in Java:

```java
import java.util.*;

public class MinimumVertexCoverInTree {
    static int[][] dp;
    static ArrayList<Integer>[] tree;

    public static int minimumVertexCover(int[] parent) {
        int n = parent.length + 1;
```

```
        dp = new int[n][2];
        tree = new ArrayList[n];
        for (int i = 0; i < n; i++) {
            tree[i] = new ArrayList<Integer>();
        }

        // Build the tree
        for (int i = 0; i < n - 1; i++) {
            int u = parent[i];
            int v = i + 1;
            tree[u].add(v);
            tree[v].add(u);
        }

        // Initialize leaf nodes
        for (int i = 0; i < n; i++) {
            if (tree[i].size() == 1) {
                dp[i][0] = 0;
                dp[i][1] = 1;
            }
        }

        // Compute DP values bottom-up
        dfs(0, -1);

        return Math.min(dp[0][0], dp[0][1]);
    }

    static void dfs(int u, int parent) {
        for (int v : tree[u]) {
            if (v != parent) {
                dfs(v, u);
                dp[u][0] += Math.min(dp[v][0], dp[v][1]);
                dp[u][1] += dp[v][0];
            }
        }
    }

    public static void main(String[] args) {
        int[] parent = {0, 0, 1, 1, 2, 2, 3, 3, 4, 4, 5, 5, 6, 6, 7,
    7};
        int ans = minimumVertexCover(parent);
        System.out.println(ans); // Output: 4
    }
}
```

In this example, we represent the tree as an array 'parent'
where 'parent[i]' is the parent node of node 'i'. The 'mini-
mumVertexCover' function takes this array as input and returns the minimum vertex cover size.

The 'dfs' function is a helper function that performs the depth-first search to compute the DP values. The 'dp' table is initialized with the base cases for the leaf nodes, and then the 'dfs' function is called with the root node as the starting node. For each node visited in the DFS, the DP values are computed using the recurrence described above.

Finally, the minimum of 'dp[root][0]' and 'dp[root][1]' is returned as the overall minimum vertex cover size.

6.18   Solve the problem of finding the Maximum Subarray Sum with a Custom Scoring Function using dynamic programming.

The problem of finding the Maximum Subarray Sum with a Custom Scoring Function can be solved by using dynamic programming. This problem is commonly known as the "Maximum Subarray Problem" or "Maximum Contiguous Subarray Problem".

The problem statement requires finding the subarray within an array that has the largest sum. In this variation, we have to apply a custom scoring function to find the largest sum. The scoring function may include weighted or penalized values for certain elements in the subarray.

To solve this problem using dynamic programming, we can use a variation of the Kadanes algorithm. The basic idea of Kadane's algorithm is to maintain two values: maximum_so_far and maximum_ending_here, where maximum_ending_here represents the maximum subarray sum ending at the current position and maximum_so_far represents the largest sum seen so far.

Here are the steps for solving this problem:

1. Initialize the maximum_so_far and maximum_ending_here values to the first element of the input array.

2. Iterate through the remaining elements of the input array.

3. At each iteration, calculate a score for the current element using the custom scoring function.

4. Calculate the maximum_ending_here value as the maximum of the current element and the sum of the current element and the maximum_ending_here value from the previous iteration.

5. Update the maximum_so_far value as the maximum of the maximum_so_far and maximum_ending_here.

6. Repeat steps 3-5 until all elements have been processed.

7. The final maximum_so_far value is the answer.

Here's how this algorithm works for an input array [1, -2, 3, 4, -5, 6]:

1. Initialize maximum_so_far = maximum_ending_here = 1

2. At iteration 2, calculate score -4, calculate maximum_ending_here = max(-2, -2-4) = -2, update maximum_so_far to 1

3. At iteration 3, calculate score 9, calculate maximum_end-

ing_here = max(3, 3-2) = 3, update maximum_so_far to 3

4. At iteration 4, calculate score 16, calculate maximum_ending_here = max(4, 4+3) = 7, update maximum_so_far to 16

5. At iteration 5, calculate score -25, calculate maximum_ending_here = max(-5, -5+7) = 2, update maximum_so_far to 16

6. At iteration 6, calculate score 36, calculate maximum_ending_here = max(6, 6+2) = 8, update maximum_so_far to 36

7. The final maximum_so_far value is 36, which is the maximum subarray sum with the custom scoring function.

Here is the Java code to implement this algorithm:

```java
public static int maxSubarraySumWithCustomScoringFunction(int[] arr)
    {
    int maxSoFar = arr[0];
    int maxEndingHere = arr[0];

    for (int i = 1; i < arr.length; i++) {
        // Calculate score for current element using custom scoring
    function
        int score = getScore(arr[i]);

        maxEndingHere = Math.max(score, score + maxEndingHere);
        maxSoFar = Math.max(maxSoFar, maxEndingHere);
    }

    return maxSoFar;
}

// Example custom scoring function
public static int getScore(int n) {
    return n * n;
}
```

In this code, 'maxSoFar' and 'maxEndingHere' represent the maximum subarray sum seen so far and the maximum subarray sum ending at the current position, respectively. The 'getScore' method calculates the score for a given element using a custom scoring function. We then use these values to update 'maxSoFar' and 'maxEndingHere' at each iteration. The final 'maxSoFar' value is returned as the answer.

Note that the time complexity of this solution is $O(n)$, where n is the length of the input array.

6.19 Implement the solution to the Optimal Multistage Graph problem with Custom Cost Functions using dynamic programming.

The Optimal Multistage Graph problem is a classic optimization problem that seeks to find the shortest path through a directed graph with multiple stages, each with different costs. This problem can be solved using dynamic programming, which allows us to compute the optimal solutions for each stage and then use those solutions to compute the overall optimal solution.

Here is an implementation of the Optimal Multistage Graph problem with Custom Cost Functions using dynamic programming in Java:

```
public class OptimalMultistageGraph {
    private static final int INF = Integer.MAX_VALUE;

    public static void shortestPath(int[][] graph, int[] costs) {
        int n = graph.length;
        int[] dp = new int[n];
        int[] path = new int[n];

        for (int i = n - 2; i >= 0; i--) {
```

```
        dp[i] = INF;
        for (int j = i + 1; j < n; j++) {
            int cost = costs[i] + graph[i][j];
            if (cost < dp[i]) {
                dp[i] = cost;
                path[i] = j;
            }
        }
    }

    int current = 0;
    while (current != n - 1) {
        System.out.print(current + " -> ");
        current = path[current];
    }
    System.out.println(n - 1);
    System.out.println("Minimum cost: " + dp[0]);
    }
}
```

In this implementation, we use the bottom-up approach to
solve the problem. We use an array 'dp' to store the minimum
cost of reaching each stage starting from the last stage, and an
array 'path' to keep track of the optimal path between stages.

The loop starts from the second-to-last stage and iterates back-
ward to the first stage. For each stage 'i', we iterate through
all possible paths from 'i' to subsequent stages 'j', and compute the cost of taking that path which is the sum of the cost
of reaching stage 'i' and the cost of the edge from 'i' to 'j'. We
then update the minimum cost and optimal path if we find a
smaller cost.

After iterating through all stages, we can print the optimal
path and the minimum cost by following the 'path' array from
the first stage to the last stage.

Here's an example usage:

```
int[][] graph = {{0, 2, 1, 3, INF, INF},
                 {INF, 0, INF, INF, 4, INF},
                 {INF, INF, 0, INF, 1, 2},
```

```
              {INF, INF, INF, 0, INF, 3},
              {INF, INF, INF, INF, 0, 1},
              {INF, INF, INF, INF, INF, 0}};
int[] costs = {0, 2, 1, 2, 5, 0};

// Compute shortest path and print result
OptimalMultistageGraph.shortestPath(graph, costs);
```

This example represents a graph with six stages and custom costs. The 'graph' matrix represents the edges between stages, where 'INF' represents no edge. The 'costs' array represents the cost of each stage. Running this program would output:

```
0 -> 2 -> 4 -> 5
Minimum cost: 4
```

This indicates that the optimal path goes from stage 0 to stage 2 (cost 2), then to stage 4 (cost 1), and finally to stage 5 (cost 1), with a total minimum cost of 4.

6.20 Solve the problem of finding the Maximum Weight Matching in a Bipartite Graph with Constraints using dynamic programming.

To solve the problem of finding the Maximum Weight Matching in a Bipartite Graph with Constraints using dynamic programming, we can use the dynamic programming approach known as the Hungarian algorithm or the Kuhn-Munkres algorithm.

The Hungarian algorithm works by first creating an adjacency matrix representation of the bipartite graph. We can then initialize a label array L and a slack array S. The label ar-

ray stores the labeling of each vertex of the bipartite graph,
while the slack array stores the difference between the minimum weight of an unmatched edge and the sum of the labels
of its endpoints.

At each iteration, the algorithm searches for an augmenting
path that increases the matching size by one. An augmenting
path is a path that starts at an unmatched vertex on one side
of the bipartite graph and ends at another unmatched vertex
on the other side of the bipartite graph. If such a path exists,
we can increase the matching size by 1 by alternately flipping
the matching status of edges along the path. If no augmenting
path exists, we update the labels of the vertices and try again
until we find an augmenting path or we determine that no more
paths exist.

The algorithm terminates when no more augmenting paths are
found. At this point, the matched vertices give us the solution
to the maximum weight matching problem.

Here's an example implementation of the Hungarian algorithm
in Java:

```java
public class MaximumWeightMatching {
    private static final int INF = Integer.MAX_VALUE;

    private int[][] graph;
    private int[] labelX, labelY;
    private int[] matchX, matchY;
    private int[] slack;
    private boolean[] visitedX, visitedY;
    private int n;

    public MaximumWeightMatching(int[][] graph) {
        n = graph.length;
        this.graph = graph;
        labelX = new int[n];
        labelY = new int[n];
        matchX = new int[n];
        matchY = new int[n];
        slack = new int[n];
        visitedX = new boolean[n];
```

```java
        visitedY = new boolean[n];
        Arrays.fill(matchX, -1);
        Arrays.fill(matchY, -1);
        Arrays.fill(slack, INF);
    }

    private void updateLabels() {
        int delta = INF;
        for (int i = 0; i < n; i++) {
            if (!visitedX[i]) {
                delta = Math.min(delta, slack[i]);
            }
        }
        for (int i = 0; i < n; i++) {
            if (visitedX[i]) {
                labelX[i] += delta;
            }
            if (visitedY[i]) {
                labelY[i] -= delta;
            } else {
                slack[i] -= delta;
            }
        }
    }

    private boolean dfs(int x) {
        visitedX[x] = true;
        for (int y = 0; y < n; y++) {
            if (visitedY[y]) {
                continue;
            }
            int gap = labelX[x] + labelY[y] - graph[x][y];
            if (gap == 0) {
                visitedY[y] = true;
                if (matchY[y] == -1 || dfs(matchY[y])) {
                    matchX[x] = y;
                    matchY[y] = x;
                    return true;
                }
            } else {
                slack[y] = Math.min(slack[y], gap);
            }
        }
        return false;
    }

    public int maximumWeightMatching() {
        for (int i = 0; i < n; i++) {
            for (int j = 0; j < n; j++) {
                labelX[i] = Math.max(labelX[i], graph[i][j]);
            }
        }
        for (int i = 0; i < n; i++) {
```

```
        while (true) {
            Arrays.fill(visitedX, false);
            Arrays.fill(visitedY, false);
            Arrays.fill(slack, INF);
            if (dfs(i)) {
                break;
            } else {
                updateLabels();
            }
        }
    }
    int result = 0;
    for (int i = 0; i < n; i++) {
        if (matchX[i] != -1) {
            result += graph[i][matchX[i]];
        }
    }
    return result;
    }
}
```

In the example above, the constructor receives the adjacency matrix of the bipartite graph, and the 'maximumWeightMatching()' method returns the maximum weight matching in the graph. The algorithm uses the 'dfs()' method to search for augmenting paths and the 'updateLabels()' method to update the labeling of the vertices. The labeling is updated by finding the smallest slack value for all vertices that are not yet matched and adding this value to the labels of the vertices that have already been visited. The 'maximumWeightMatching()' method initializes the label arrays and then iteratively searches for augmenting paths until no more paths exist. It then computes the total weight of the matching and returns this value as the solution.

Printed in Great Britain
by Amazon

41275563R00145